the series on school

Patricia A. Wasley	Ann Lieberman
University of Washington	Carnegie Foundation for Advancement of Teaching

SERIES EDITORS

the series on school reform, *continued*

Teachers in Professional Communities

Improving Teaching and Learning

Ann Lieberman
and
Lynne Miller, Editors

Teachers College, Columbia University
New York and London

Published by Teachers College Press, 1234 Amsterdam Avenue, New York, NY 10027

Library of Congress Cataloging-in-Publication Data

Teachers in professional communities : improving teaching and learning / Ann Lieberman, Lynne Miller, editors.
     p. cm. — (Series on school reform)
   Includes bibliographical references and index.
   ISBN 978-0-8077-4889-3 (pbk. : alk. paper) —
   ISBN 978-0-8077-4890-9 (hardcover : alk. paper)
   1. Teachers—Training of—United States. I. Lieberman, Ann. II. Miller, Lynne, 1945–
   LB1025.3.T43 2008
   370.71'5—dc22   2008011752

ISBN 978-0-8077-4889-3 (paper)
ISBN 978-0-8077-4890-9 (cloth)

Printed on acid-free paper
Manufactured in the United States of America

15   14   13   12   11   10   09   08   8   7   6   5   4   3   2   1

Contents

v

Introduction

Ann Lieberman
Lynne Miller

This is a book about professional learning communities and their potential for improving teaching and learning for both the adults and students in our schools. It is clear to us that the changes that schools need to embrace now and in the future require invention, adaptation, and a new sense of community; they depend on strategies for professional learning that are long-term and collaborative; and they necessitate enabling policies that are shaped by those constituencies that are involved in the routines of schools and have an investment in their renewal.

It has been 30 years since we edited our first book together and used the term "staff development" to connote a new and somewhat daring way to look at improving teaching; we aimed to challenge traditional notions of teacher training and in-service education. Since then we have seen ideas about teacher development, our own included, critiqued and modified (Borko, 2004). As educators and policymakers continue to focus on teacher professional development as a strategy for school reform, they persist in launching ambitious efforts to reach ambitious goals that, not surprisingly, fail to meet desired ends. The real life of school, with its inherent contradictions, ongoing routines, and unrelenting dailiness intervenes; and the best of intentions fail to materialize as planned. What accounts for this disconnect between the promise and the performance of staff development as a reform strategy? Why do so many policies that are based on the best available research and knowledge fail to deliver? Why aren't programs that focus on improvements in content knowledge and teaching techniques enough? We believe that the answers to these questions lie in a major conceptual flaw that underpins the work; that is to say, there is a mistaken belief that teachers can increase their effectiveness and deepen their practice outside of the professional communities to which they belong. Such a belief has led to a bifurcation between professional development policies that mandate and those that build competence, between supporting individual growth and the growth of teaching communities.

Based on our own and others' research and practice, we have come to believe that professional learning communities provide a fundamentally different and promising way to think about how teachers can deepen their practice and improve their craft in support of student learning. Defined as *ongoing groups of teachers who meet regularly for the purpose of increasing their own learning and that of their students,* professional learning communities offer an environment where new ideas and strategies emerge, take root, and develop; and where competence can truly be cultivated and nurtured. Some of these communities take hold within schools; others cross school, district, or sometimes state boundaries; others focus on a particular discipline, grade level or way of thinking about teaching; still others include a heterogeneous mix of people from multiple contexts and disciplines.

Though difficult to form, professional learning communities can lead to authentic changes in teaching practice and improved student learning. Such communities challenge long-held ideas about how teachers learn; they enact professional development in nontraditional ways; and they position teachers as the leaders of their own professional growth and development (Lieberman & Miller, 2007; Little & Curry, 2008; McLaughlin & Talbert, 2001; Seashore, Kruse, & Marks, 1996). Because they focus on the relationships that occur between and among principals, teachers, peers, students, and content, these communities reverse the isolation of teachers that begins in pre-service training and often continues throughout the teaching career. They provide a place for teachers to work together and connect with one another about their own work and the work of their students. They afford opportunities for engagement in joint work, critical reflection, and problem solving that is aimed at individual, collective, and schoolwide improvements in curriculum, instruction, and organization. In short, professional learning communities bring people into an environment where colleagues work together on the everyday tensions of teaching. In many cases, these communities lead to a transformation in teacher identity; members move from seeing themselves as "just a teacher" to being part of a larger community where new practices are constantly being created and learned rather than a fixed menu.

When we began to think about writing this book we reviewed the research literature, as good academics always do. But we knew that was not enough. We wanted to learn from the field, as well, and draw on the real life experience of people who actually initiated and grew teaching communities. So we created a book that equally privileges research and practice. We worked hard to show why they are both needed to understand professional learning communities. And throughout we wanted to emphasize that these communities are most successful when they wed the development of teaching competence to the development of teaching community.

Part One takes the form of an extended essay in three chapters, in which we review and synthesize findings from current research and development about professional learning communities. Part Two focuses on case studies, written by educators who led in the creation and the realization of such communities. We found it useful to look at all of the studies and cases through the lens of five organizing themes—*Context, Commitment, Capacity, Content,* and *Challenge*—and to ask: What difference does context make? Why does context matter? How do communities build commitment from their members? What kind of commitments do members make? How do members develop the capacity to collaborate with and learn from one another? What new capacities do groups build in their members? How do communities deal with the competing agendas of content and process issues? What happens when they do not? And last, what common challenges emerge from these separate narratives of professional communities?

As with all our collaborations, we have grown through the process—learning from one another, rewriting one another's work, clarifying one another's ideas, and struggling to get it right. Read on and join us in the struggle to know, to understand, and to learn why professional learning communities that join competence with community hold such promise for our teachers and the students in their care.

PART I

Learning from Research and Development

1

Contexts and Commitments

Ann Lieberman
Lynne Miller

Like all phenomena, professional learning communities are embedded within a context. In this case, the context is the long history of staff development as it has evolved. In the United States, teacher staff development has its roots in the late 1950s and early 1960s when Congress passed the National Defense and Education Act (NDEA) in response to the Soviet launch of Sputnik. Intended to close the perceived gap between Soviet and American achievement in science and technology, NDEA inserted public schools into the arena of Cold War national defense. Teachers were viewed as foot soldiers in need of retraining for a new mission, and universities were recruited to take charge of the assignment. Higher education faculties were funded to develop scripted, "teacher-proof" curriculum in math, science, and foreign languages. Not surprisingly, the universities implemented what they knew best. Professors taught in their areas of expertise in discipline-specific summer institutes; and students (in this case teachers) were instructed to absorb the new information, ideas, and materials that were being transmitted and then apply them to their classrooms in the fall. The institutes represented the first major national effort to reform schools from the outside, using teacher staff development as its strategy.

A few years later, the Elementary and Secondary Education Act (ESEA) of 1965 was passed. Just as the NDEA had placed the schools in a national defense role, the ESEA positioned them as agents of social change. As before, external experts were charged with the development and dissemination of curriculum materials and strategies that teachers were expected to adopt with high degrees of fidelity. In both NDEA and ESEA we saw the establishment of a training model of staff development.

This model has enjoyed a long life. It still flourishes in the form of in-service days, one-time workshops, short-term institutes, and—more recently—in training teachers to implement "scientifically based practices." Kennedy (1998), in a review of the literature of staff development in science and mathematics, found that norm was the transmission of knowledge by experts. She identified four categories of staff development programs: (1) those that prescribed a set of teaching behaviors that are expected to apply generically to all school subjects; (2) those that prescribed a set of teaching behaviors that seem generic, but were proffered as applying to one particular school subject, such as mathematics or science; (3) those that provided general guidance on both curriculum and pedagogy for teaching a particular subject and that justified their recommended practices with references to knowledge about how students learn this subject; and (4) those that provided knowledge about how students learn particular subject matter but did not provide specific guidance on the practices that should be used to teach that subject.

Over the decades, myriad scholars (Corcoran, 1995; Goldenberg & Gallimore, 1991; Hammond, 1998; Hammond & McLaughlin, 1995; Lieberman & Miller, 2007; Little, 1993; Loucks-Horsley, 1998) have advocated for alternative approaches. Too often, these alternatives have been diluted. Instead of representing fundamentally different conceptions of teaching, teacher knowledge, and teacher growth, they became one of several options on a diverse menu. As an example, on its website the National Staff Development Council lists the following as effective learning strategies: action research, coaching, content-specific workshops, examining student work, lesson study, mentoring, observing classrooms, study groups, technology, walk-throughs, and general workshops. At the same time, the Council defines staff development as programmatic activities that are designed by leaders who "select learning strategies based on the intended outcomes and their diagnosis of participants' prior knowledge and experience." The Council further states, "To promote the development of new instructional skills, training may be combined with coaching, study groups, and action research" (National Staff Development Council, nd). The idea of staff development as training designed by outside experts dies hard.

Our goal here and in the next three chapters in Part One is to focus on what research has to say about teacher professional learning communities as a new and promising approach to teacher development and to unravel their complexities and potentials from a research and development perspective. We seek to define what such communities are and what they are not and to articulate their signature theories and practices. Instead of developing a traditional review of the literature, we focus on a small number of research studies. While we acknowledge that these sources are highly selective and that they do not begin to capture the breadth and depth of the research, we think that they provide an excellent starting place for uncovering what we know about professional learning communities. The studies are listed below by author:

- Milbrey McLaughlin and Joan Talbert (2001). A large-scale study of departments at a range of high schools where weak, strong-traditional, and strong-innovative teacher communities were in place.

- Pam Grossman, Sam Wineburg, and Stephen Woolworth (2001). A single case study of the first 18 months of the formation and early development of the Humanities Group, a community of teachers of history and English who came together to develop a new humanities curriculum.
- Judith Little and Ilana Horn (2007) and Ilana Horn (2005). A collection of studies that were part of a longer research project on the professional development of a long-lived group of California math teachers. Called the Algebra Study Group, they met regularly to discuss mathematics and the teaching of math.
- Ann Lieberman and Diane Wood (2002). A description and analysis of how teachers learned together about writing—their own and that of their students—in Oklahoma and California, two sites of the National Writing Project.
- The National School Reform Faculty (1998). A video representation of a Critical Friends Group (CFG) in which cross curricular groups of teachers meet regularly to look at their own and students' work.
- Marilyn Cochran-Smith and Susan Lytle (1993). A description and analysis of Project START and National Writing Project research communities in Philadelphia.
- Ann Lieberman (2007). A reflection on her experiences in the professional learning communities that took hold in the Carnegie Academy for the Scholarship of Teaching and Learning (CASTL).
- Lynne Miller (2007). A retrospective examination of the development of professional learning communities within the Southern Maine Partnership, a school–university collaboration that she has directed for 20 years.

Each of the studies in our review locates professional learning communities within specific contexts. Our first understanding is that context matters. It influences how communities emerge and develop, how they forge commitments, build capacity, and deal with issues of content and process. And, they have a major impact on the challenges and tensions that emerge along the way. Below, we provide a description of the context of each of the studies included in our review.

CONTEXTS OF THE RESEARCH STUDIES

The high school departments in the McLaughlin and Talbert (2001) study involved 22 schools from multiple state, district, and school contexts. The sample was taken from two states, California and Michigan. Seven school districts were represented; also included were three independent schools and two special mission public schools. There were two very different policy milieus at the state level, with Michigan being decentralized while California was highly centralized. The seven districts had diverse stances toward innovation and reform and could be categorized as either "moving" or "stuck" (p. 157). At the school level, there were differences in principal leadership, subject matter orthodoxies, and the mission of the schools. Principals set the stage for the kind of teacher communities that emerged through the relationships they established with teachers and students and the way they allocated resources and provided support. Subject matter departments, with distinct and content-driven ways of talking about students, content, and pedagogy, created communities with very different norms and expectations of members. The missions of the schools, which made public the values and practices they espoused, ran a wide gamut as well. All of these contextual factors contributed to the professional communities that developed, which the researches labeled as weak communities, strong-traditional communities, or strong-innovative communities.

The Humanities Group involved 22 English and history teachers in one high school. Pam Grossman, Sam Wineburg, and Stephen Woolworth convened the group themselves as part of a staff development project aimed at crafting an interdisciplinary curriculum. They then studied the group's formation as they facilitated its work. The researchers stated, "We created a 'community of teacher learners by declaration' and invited teachers to join us" (Grossman, Wineburg, & Woolworth, 2001, p. 949). While the participants were all nominally volunteers, several were pressed into participation by their department heads while others were motivated to join by the generous stipend that was offered. The researchers noted that they "saw ourselves as something of a cross between 'project organizers' and 'project leaders,'" and that they and the department heads "set the initial frame for the meetings" (p. 950). The context of the group's formation, as well as its design and leadership, set the stage for many of the benchmark issues it faced over the first 18 months of its existence.

Though also located in one high school, the Algebra Study Group had very different beginnings and existed within a very different context. Initiated by teachers and based on volunteer participation, it had been meeting for several years before it came under the scrutiny of the researchers. East High School, the home of the group, had a long history of reform leadership emanating from the departments in general and from the math department in particular. The teachers had control over hiring and sought out colleagues who were committed to their shared values of "collective work on curriculum and teaching" (Horn, 2005, p. 213). In addition, the school culture privileged classroom practice over school-wide reform in its improvement efforts. This context, characterized by teacher empowerment within departments and a focus on teaching and learning at the classroom level, provided the conditions for the development and continuation of an autonomous professional community of teachers of mathematics.

The contexts within which the professional communities of the National Writing Project developed and took root were very different from those described above. Designated as formal sites within a national network and located on two university campuses (the University of California at Los Angeles and Oklahoma State University), they began with a set of assumptions and practices that had been crafted over the 30-year history of the project.

Assumptions included a firm belief in the power of school–university partnerships and in the ability of teachers to reform teaching and schools, a trust in the efficacy of teachers teaching one another, and a commitment to teachers as writers and critics of one another's writing. Sites followed a common process of nomination, invitation, and voluntary participation of members. This process ensured that each site could "bring together teachers who had built reputations for strong, effective teaching" and who chose to engage in the work (Lieberman & Wood, 2002, p. 15).

The Critical Friends Groups (CFGs) were part of the National School Reform Faculty (NSRF), a national network that defines itself as "a professional development initiative that focuses on developing collegial relationships, encouraging reflective practice, and rethinking leadership in restructuring schools—all in support of increased student achievement." CFGs were limited in size to 8 to 12 volunteer members who met for about 2 hours at least once a month, used "proven structures and practices," and convened under the leadership of trained facilitators (http://www.nsrfharmony.org/mission. html). The CFG that was recorded in the NSRF video project (National School Reform Faculty, 1998) was located in a newly constructed school that followed the principles of the Coalition of Essential Schools, and where participation in an ongoing CFG was a condition of hire.

Project START was a learning community that " invites student teachers into a community of learners and as a way of life as teachers by emphasizing reform, research, and renewal across the professional life span" (Cochran-Smith & Lytle, 1993, p. 66). The communities developed around a 12-month postbaccalaureate teacher preparation program that involved student teachers and cooperating teachers who were involved in other collaboratives and research communities. In addition, university supervisors and faculty members participated. Members met weekly in teacher research communities where they inquired into issues of "language and literacy; curriculum and pedagogy; race, class, and gender; modes of assessment; and cultures of schools and teaching" (p. 67). They had the opportunity to document processes, engage in critical discussion, and prepare collaborative analyses—all within the context of other teacher research communities, many of which had been meeting for over 20 years. Project START's embeddedness in an established culture of teacher inquiry and community informed much of its trajectory as a professional learning community.

The CASTL Project was developed under the auspices of The Carnegie Foundation for the Advancement of Teaching (CFAT). The project was originally designed to bring teachers and teacher educators together in learning communities with the goal of developing "a scholarship of teaching to improve student learning, enhance the practice and profession of teaching, and bring to teaching the recognition and reward afforded to other forms of scholarly work." The project began to consider ways to help teachers go public with their practice and open it up to feedback and reflection. The result was the "Carnegie Foundation Gallery of Teaching and Learning: Going Public with Teaching" project, in which teachers designed digital exhibitions of their work that were published on a website (see www. insideteaching.org).

The Southern Maine Partnership was established in 1985 as a school–university collaboration dedicated to improving teaching and teacher education. As such, it provided the context for the cultivation of school–university learning communities for over 20 years and also nurtured the development of multiple teacher communities that took root within and across member districts. By establishing a forum that crossed institutional boundaries, the Partnership helped to advance a regional culture that supported collegial conversation, collective inquiry, and reciprocal assistance. The communities that arose in this environment were strengthened by its support and yet were vulnerable to the ebb and flow of the Partnership as an organization.

FORGING COMMITMENTS

Just as contexts differ, so do the paths that communities take in forging and maintaining the commitment of their members. No two professional learning communities are the same; each is unique, generating its own path of development and finding its own ways to build community identities and to learn from other communities.

There is no such thing as an instant community, nor is there a single template for its form and content. It takes time for a community to take hold and for its members to develop effective ways to talk, think, and learn together. As Grossman, Wineburg, and Woolworth (2001) noted, teachers have to get to know one another as thinkers and learners before they can embark on a common enterprise and grapple with difficult issues, and they need time to develop ways of working together effectively.

There are myriad ways that professional learning communities initiate the process of getting to know one another. The Humanities Group began with a book group that read three short texts and talked about them in response to two framing questions. The National Writing Project had all new members attend its Invitational Summer Institute, an intensive 5-week experience. A summer institute was also the starting point for the teacher-scholars in CASTL, while Southern Maine Partnership groups began with monthly dinner meetings over texts and common concerns. Critical Friends Groups formed in a variety of ways and were, more often than not, school-based. Project START, a teacher research community in Philadelphia, brought together interns and experienced teachers. The interns initally met as a group centered on common coursework and field placements and later were invited to join monthly seminars with experienced teachers and mentors.

In all instances, the initial meetings were meant to build a commitment to the emerging community. This approach was particularly successful in the National Writing Project, where the experience was

> so powerful that, within 5 weeks, strangers from different kinds of schools and
> often without shared backgrounds or beliefs, come together and, as a group,
> share their practices with one another, write and present something them-

selves, critique one another's work, give constructive feedback to their peers on their writing, read and discuss research and contemporary literature, and become part of a community of fellow teachers who accept improving one's practice as a norm for being a teacher. (Lieberman & Wood, 2002, p. 35)

In other cases, success was not so immediate. The Humanities Group, which initially floundered, is a case in point. While Pam Grossman, Sam Wineburg, and Stephen Woolworth, as organizers and facilitators of the group, had hoped that a discussion of common texts would lead to full and active participation, quite the opposite occurred. The group had difficulty sustaining a conversation; some teachers dominated, and others remained silent. At the end of the first group meeting, Grossman, Wineburg, and Woolworth (2001) reported, "As project facilitators, we were left scratching our heads, wondering what went wrong" (p. 955).

As they facilitated and observed the group over time, Grossman, Wineburg, and Woolworth observed how members met and overcame this and other obstacles to community development. They developed a model of the formation of teacher professional communities that identified four benchmarks of community growth: the formation of group identity, navigating fault lines, negotiating the essential tension, and communal responsibility for individual growth. For each marker, there are indictors of beginning, evolving, and mature communities as represented in Table 1.1.

While this model is specific to the Humanities Group, it offers insight into the benchmarks that teacher communities encounter as they move from a collection of individuals to a cohesive and committed group of learners.

Committing to Community Identities

Teachers in professional learning communities develop new identities as group members. Wenger (1991) noted that communities of practice contribute to construction of identities. In the National Writing Project, a participant explained her identity as a group member this way.

Well, I think number one is that if I'm a teacher of writing, I have to be a writer. That's, I guess, the biggest idea. If I'm going to be a teacher of reading, I have to be a reader. . . . Then, the next step I learned was I need to share my teaching with other teachers. And now I know I have some good ideas that other people would like to hear about. (Lieberman & Wood, 2002, p. 20)

These multiple identities—a writer, a teacher of writing, a reader, a teacher of reading, and a teacher of teachers— were forged within the community of the local National Writing Project site.

Identity formation of new members is vital to the survival of professional communities. According to Wenger (1998), newcomers learn to become parts of a community of practice through "legitimate peripheral participation." As part of this process, group members engage in extended conversations that

Table 1.1. Model of the Formation of Teacher Professional Community

Beginning	Evolving	Mature
1. Formation of Group Identity and Norms of Interaction		
• Identification with subgroups • Individuals are interchangeable and expendable • Undercurrent of incivility • Sense of individualism overrides responsibility to group norms	• Pseudocommunity • Recognition of unique contributions of individual members • Open discussion of interactional norms • Recognition of need to regulate group behavior	• Identification with whole group • Recognition that group is enriched by multiple perspectives • Developing new interactional norms • Communal responsibility for and regulation of behavior
2. Navigating Fault Lines		
• Denial of difference • Conflict goes backstage	• Appropriation of difference by dominant position • Conflict erupts onto main stage and feared	• Understanding and productive use of difference • Conflict is expected feature of group life and dealt with openly and honestly
3. Negotiating the Essential Tension		
• Lack of agreement over purposes of professional community	• Begrudging willingness to let different people pursue different activities	• Recognition that teacher learning and student learning are fundamentally intertwined
4. Communal Responsibility for Individual Growth		
• Belief that teachers' responsibility to students' intellectual growth is an individual responsibility • Contributions to group are acts of individual volition	• Recognition that colleagues can be resources for one's learning • Recognition that participation is expected	• Commitment to colleagues' growth • Acceptance of rights of individuals and group obligations

Source: Adapted from Grossman, Wineburg, & Woolworth (2001).

allow them to make transparent their reasoning about their professional practices and how they frame problems. New members absorb

> how masters of their trade talk, walk, work, and generally conduct their lives; how people who are not part of the community or practice interact with it; what other newcomers are doing; what newcomers need to learn to become full practitioners; increasing understanding of how, when, and what about old-timers collaborate, collude, and collide and what they enjoy, dislike, respect, and admire. (p. 98)

Algebra Study Group members were serious about their role as agents in identity formation. For example, during a "check-in" an intern teacher posed a problem of practice about the difficulty she encountered in teaching in a heterogeneous math class. She framed the problem in terms of "fast" and "slow" students and sought support from the group by asking them to suggest activities she might use in her class. Instead of offering solutions, group members focused on how the intern was talking about the students. By sharing their own experiences and thinking, they gently encouraged her to reconsider her classification of students as being "slow" and "fast" and to think about the assumptions that students might bring to their own learning and to her classroom. In the process of the conversation, the group made their pedagogic reasoning transparent, demonstrating how they talked and thought about students and learning. In doing so, they introduced the intern to the social practices of the group.

Likewise, in Project START the teacher-mentors guided the interns toward the community's norms, values, and practices. The teacher-mentors were

> expected to bring an inquiry-centered perspective to their roles as mentors and to articulate their own questions and frameworks to student teachers as they support students' initial forays into inquiry. (Cochran-Smith & Lytle, 1993, p. 68)

These expectations are very different from those occurring in traditional induction programs, where the role of mentors is to teach newcomers the rules of the organization and how to follow them. In Project START, mentors were called upon to model and impart interrogations and challenges of existing beliefs and practices. They constructed inquiry projects that were specifically designed to bring the intern teachers into the fold as teacher-researchers and provide entry into the community.

Committing to Learning from Peers

As teachers learn from one another they begin to see the ways that group members can contribute to and enrich one another's development and growth. With this realization comes a deeper commitment to community membership. The idea that learning occurs within peer interactions was first introduced by Jean Lave, an anthropologist, and Etienne Wenger, an expert in artificial intelligence, in an effort to describe how learning occurred within groups that shared a common purpose. Learning, they argued, does not result from individual cognitive processes nor from direct teaching; rather, it is the result of the social interactions that are part of participation in daily life as members of communities of practice. Wenger explains,

> A community of practice is not merely a club of friends or a network of connections between people. It has an identity defined by a shared domain of interest. Membership therefore implies a commitment to the domain, and therefore a shared competence that distinguishes members from other people. . . . In pursuing their interest in their domain, members engage in joint activities and discussions, help one another, and share information. They build relationships that enable them to learn from [one another]. (Wenger, nd)

Communities of practice are about much more than what works in terms of technical skills and knowledge; they are about what matters in terms of shared experiences. And learning is not about what happens in people's heads; it is about what happens in their relationships and conversations with others who are engaged in common work.

Wenger defines a community of practice as having three dimensions: a purpose or joint enterprise, social practices, and a shared repertoire. He notes that members of these communities "develop a shared repertoire of resources: experiences, stories, tools, ways of addressing recurring problems—in short a shared practice. This takes time and sustained interaction" (Wenger, nd, http://www.ewenger.com/theory).

McLaughlin and Talbert (2001) provide evidence of how these three dimensions were enacted in the high schools they studied. The researchers categorize teaching communities as either "enacting tradition," "lowering expectations and standards," or "innovating to engage students." In the first instance, the community viewed its purpose as managing content and maintaining subject matter integrity. They adopted social practices that were grounded in the belief that poor student outcomes were the result of student attributes and not of teaching practices. The teaching repertoire maintained conventional classroom routines that focused on transmitting knowledge, despite their ineffectiveness. According to McLaughlin and Talbert (2001), in this kind of community, teachers

> refuse to abandon the core principles of the profession, which hold teachers responsible for sustaining the integrity of the discipline as formalized curriculum and certifying student mastery of course content and subject area skills. (p. 22)

The second type of community works from a different set of purposes, though its social practices are based on a similar assumption that the responsibility for poor student outcomes lies with the students and not the teacher. These communities chose to modify the traditional curriculum for the students that they judged to be less able. They took as their mission to maintain order and quiet and to help students get by with minimal effort and challenge. Teaching practices that diluted the curriculum and taught less content were the norm.

Teachers in the third category of community reject the idea that students need traditional content taught in traditional ways and refuse to dilute learning opportunities in order to keep the peace. Rather, teachers in this kind of community embrace the goal of reaching every student and realize that they would be "changing practices to match students' learning styles" (McLaughlin & Talbert, 2001, p. 32). The shared teaching repertoire includes a wide range of practices, from chalkboard instruction to hands-on activities, cooperative learning groups, and project work.

2

Developing Capacities

Ann Lieberman
Lynne Miller

As teachers make commitments to their professional learning communities, they simultaneously develop new ways of talking and thinking. They learn to move from congenial to collegial conversation and to take part in honest talk. They develop the ability and disposition to do knowledge work and engage with theory and research as well as with practice. They become skilled at making connections among their profession, their teaching practices, and the learning of their students. They gain the confidence to go public with their work, and they enlarge their ideas about what it means to be a teacher. In doing so, they also redefine the role of teacher.

THE CAPACITY FOR HONEST TALK

Professional learning communities are collegial cultures where teachers develop the capacity to engage in honest talk. There is a big difference between congeniality and collegiality. Congeniality is marked by relationships that are amiable and compatible but, more often than not, are also conflict- and risk-adverse. In congenial cultures, teachers become comfortable with sharing stories, making reassurances, and placing blame on outside forces they view as beyond their control. In their eagerness to maintain likability, members skirt around issues of disagreement and potential conflict. Collegial cultures, on the other hand, develop bonds of trust among members that transcend congeniality. They provide a forum for reflection and honest feedback, for challenge and disagreement, and for accepting responsibility without assigning blame.

Collegial groups stand in marked contrast to traditional school cultures that value individualism, isolation, and privacy. They are also dissimilar from groups that may on the surface appear to be collegial, but on closer view are not. Such communities are more apt to be "playing community" (Grossman, Wineburg, & Woolworth, 2001) than enacting it. Hargreaves (1991) coined the term "contrived collegiality" to describe such groups; Grossman, Wineburg, and Woolworth used the term "pseudo-community" to describe the same phenomena. They pinpointed the suppression of conflict as the identifying trait:

> Groups regulate face to face interactions with the tacit understanding that it is "against the rules" to challenge others or press too hard for clarification. This understanding paves the way for the illusion of consensus. (p. 955)

In collegial cultures, on the other hand, group members move beyond consensus, they resist giving one another reassurance or quick fixes, and they go deeper to uncover and analyze problems.

Each professional learning community has specific practices that sustain relationships and open dialogue. The Algebra Group built collegiality through the "check in," a time at the beginning of each meeting where members were invited to present a problem or a new idea for the group to consider. In the National Writing Project, participants relied on the "author's chair" as a way to present their work as teachers and as writers, and to elicit feedback and critique. The members of the Critical Friends Groups (CFGs) depended on a set of protocols to guide discussion and elicit "warm and cool" feedback. And in the teacher research communities, teachers employed journals, oral inquiries, classroom studies, and essays as ways of establishing collaborative relationships.

The capacity to engage in honest and disclosing talk cannot be underestimated in professional learning communities. This kind of talk requires a commitment to time and to the conditions that support collegiality and trust. Conversation was key in the formation and continuation of Southern Maine Partnership groups. As group memberships became stable, the talk became more honest and focused. In the Algebra Group, talk was the vehicle for "normalizing" problems of classroom practice, and the talk became generative of learning because it invited "disclosure of and reflection on problems of practice"(Little & Horn, 2007, p. 50).

The video documentary of an interdisciplinary high school CFG showed the power of honest talk. The video showed a math teacher as she presented a problem of practice to other group members. The teacher began by explaining the difficulty her students were having in articulating in writing the process they used to solve mathematical problems. After the teacher presented her dilemma, the group members asked clarifying questions, followed by more probing questions:

Have you been a model for what you want?
How did you get them to the point they are able to do this?
Do you write on the board what you want them to do on paper?

After the math teacher responded, the following conversation took place.

> *CFG Member:* You're asking kids to document how they get an answer. And maybe they can't do this because you can't do it. You can't document the results from changes you make and they can't do the same thing. . . .
> (Strained silence)
> . . . Know what I mean? Maybe you'll learn how to do it by teaching them to do it.
> (Laughter and smiles all round)
> *Math teacher:* How they do and talk it through?
> *CFG Member:* Yes.
> *Math teacher:* Got some wheels spinning.

This level of disclosure and feedback is what we mean by honest talk or what Little and Horn (2007) call "consequential conversations." These interactions go far beyond the congeniality of most teacher groups and are a marker of a mature professional learning community.

THE CAPACITY TO DO KNOWLEDGE WORK

For most teachers, theory and research are considered irrelevant, if not useless. As Hargreaves (1984) noted, for teachers, "Experience counts, theory doesn't" (p. 244). Yet, the construction and application of new knowledge is very much a part of teaching. In fact, teachers are always working from tacit knowledge and implicit theories that they often don't recognize as such. In professional learning communities, teachers develop the capacity to become self-conscious knowledge workers—that is, people who generate and manipulate knowledge. They begin with experience, but they work their way toward theory. *Reflective practice*, a term coined by Schön in the 1950s, is an apt descriptor of this process. Schön, an urban planner who had become wary of the technical rationality that so dominated thinking about organizational learning, sought a more adequate way to describe how professionals learn and think about their craft. Chief among the ideas he proposed are *reflection-in-action* and *reflection-on-action*. The first, reflection-in-action, is a form of "thinking on our feet." When a professional reflects-in-action, she behaves like a scientist, engaged in an experiment in which she is the subject. By looking at her own behaviors and responses to a situation, she can generate hypotheses and new understandings about herself in the situation; this is how she engages in learning.

Reflection-on-action takes place after the action has occurred and engages the professional in writing up what occurred or talking things through with a colleague. Such collegial conversations lead to new questions and ideas about practice, frame learning, and guide future actions.

Reflective practice leads to the development of a repertoire: a collection of images, ideas, actions, and metaphors that a person develops and draws upon to understand new situations, make predictions, and guide new actions. With a well-developed repertoire, the professional creates mental maps that allow her to see what is both familiar and unfamiliar in a new situation. When professionals work collaboratively to define and resolve problems, they also develop shared mental maps. These maps comprise what Schön (1983) calls "theory-in-use"—the practically constructed ideas that guide actions. Professionals depend on theory-in-use to a greater extent than those theories that are formally learned or espoused. Reflective practice leads to learning that is reciprocal, practical, active, and open to revision.

In the Algebra Study Group, individuals used reflection-in-action as they went about the task of teaching their students in their individual classrooms. Reflection-on-action occurred later, during the "check in." In one such instance, a teacher presented the problem she encountered when she introduced manipulatives to her students. As other group members became engaged, they went back and forth between the problem posed and their own experiences of practice. In doing so, they collaboratively reframed their images of classroom practice and

> they could collectively construct a class of instances and narrated responses that are clustered round defining and explaining a common teaching problem and a set of principles for responding. (Little & Horn, 2007, np)

Group members continued to define and redefine their shared repertoire and develop a common theory-in-use.

Schön (1983) emphasized that reflective practice is not unidirectional and that professional knowledge does not flow from the expert to student. In his view, "The movement of learning is as much from periphery to periphery, or from periphery to centre, as from centre to periphery" rather than being limited to "the nexus of official policies at the centre" (p. 165).

Cochran-Smith and Lytle (1993) added to this idea of how learning takes place when they introduced the concept of "inside/outside knowledge" in their description of how teachers from Philadelphia research communities engaged in inquiry about their practice. Inside/outside knowledge challenges the common assumption that university researchers are in the best position to discover and codify knowledge about teaching. It is

> a juxtaposition intended to call attention to teachers as knowers and to the complex and distinctly nonlinear relationships of knowledge and teaching as they are embedded in the contexts and the relations of power that structure the daily work of teachers and learners in both the school and the university. (p. xi)

Teacher-as-knower is a recurrent theme in all the groups we looked at. CASTL positions teachers as scholars of their own practice. The National

Writing Project starts with the assumption that teachers bring an abundance of craft knowledge to their work, and this knowledge is the building block for increased learning through collaboration. One teacher participant was quoted as saying,

> We need what other people know. And this could be the person sitting next to us in the summer institute, or the teacher down the hall. . . . It's about starting with where everyone is and what they know about teaching and their field and acknowledging that to learn, we need to find our own answers together. And part of that is simply by listening. (Lieberman & Wood, 2002, p. 23)

Much of current professional development activity rests on the assumption that there are best practices *out there.* In professional learning communities, this belief is replaced by the conviction that the best practices are *in here;* they can be uncovered by mining inside knowledge. The CFGs relied on a set of protocols to guide discussions under the leadership of a teacher-facilitator, called a coach. Each protocol took about an hour to complete and provided dedicated times for a teacher to present a concern, for group members to offer feedback and suggestions by drawing on their own knowledge and experience, for the presenter to respond to the feedback, and for the group to debrief the process. In a reflective essay, a CFG coach described how inside knowledge was called upon in his group:

> Using established structures like the "tuning protocol" and the "consultancy," we tackle problems with individual students, with program approaches, with assignments that produced poorer than expected work, with relationships as teaming professionals, and ultimately with our own mindsets and expectations. (Appleby, 1998, p. 11)

The protocols allowed teachers to dig deeply into their own knowledge base as a way to help a colleague resolve issues that emerged from practice.

But inside teacher knowledge is not enough; even the best learning communities become stale when they are closed to outside knowledge. In the National Writing Project's summer institute, teachers choose a research question to pursue and spend a significant amount of time in the library and on the Internet. In doing so, they refresh their interests in professional literature. One past participant remarked that she had lost sight of the value of reading beyond her own class assignments, but regained the habit as a result of the institute: "I learned through the reading and now . . . I buy the journals myself and do a lot more reading on my own" (Lieberman & Wood, 2002, p. 16).

The CFGs also turned to outside knowledge. In fact, they regularly read articles using protocols called "The Text Based Seminar" and "The Final Word." These protocols structured time and opportunity for each group member to refer to a passage from the text and to then enlarge upon it in terms of their own insights and experiences.

Algebra Study Group members used an "Algebra Binder" that included both homegrown and external resources as a way to expand their knowledge of mathematics. Participants in the Southern Maine Partnership groups began with regular discussions of journal articles on a specific topic. In CASTL, teachers referred to outside sources as they developed their own scholarship of teaching. The Humanities Group spent a good deal of time examining texts from the two disciplines and figuring out how to integrate them. In the teacher research communities of Project START, teachers in one group generated texts that became the assigned readings that other communities examined together. In all cases, the communities struck their own balance of inside and outside knowledge.

THE CAPACITY TO CONNECT PROFESSIONAL LEARNING WITH CLASSROOM PRACTICE AND STUDENT LEARNING

Professional learning communities could be easily dismissed if they did not help build capacity for teacher to improve student learning. McLaughlin and Talbert (2001) were the first researchers to document how the technical cultures, professional norms, and organizational practices of teacher communities directly connects to student learning. They reported that weak communities, where teacher isolation is the norm and seniority is highly valued, breed student passivity, a pedagogy based on the transmission of knowledge, and lower teacher expectations of student achievement. However, though they are more collegial and less isolating, strong-traditional communities share values and norms that do not lead to innovation and improve student outcomes. Rather, these communities enforce traditional notions of abilities, sort students into academic tracks, grade on a curve, and assign the most experienced teachers to the highest tracks and the least experienced to the lower ones. While the students in the advanced tracks are often active and engaged, those in the lower tracks are not.

The greatest gains in student achievement, according to McLaughlin and Talbert (2001), occur in strong teacher communities that focus on promoting teacher learning and connect it to student learning. What separates these communities from the strong-traditional communities is a common vision that all students are capable of increased achievement. Here teachers seek to achieve more equity in student outcomes and develop a shared language and knowledge base about how to accomplish this goal. They work together to develop practices that served all students well.

McLaughlin and Talbert (2001) go further in their analysis of strong teacher learning communities and describe the stages of their development. First is the *novice stage,* when teachers begin an inquiry process, usually by collecting data. Next is the *intermediate stage,* which starts with the realization that data are not enough and proceeds to build-broad based leadership, to focus collaborative work on clarifying goals, and developing a shared vocabulary. In the *advanced stage*, teachers deepen the inquiry process and probe more deeply into how to improve student outcomes with the goal of changing classroom instruction and generating shared reform practices. They consider the knowledge they need and use evidence to guide their investigations. In doing so, they develop a sense of collective responsibility for students' successes, show mutual respect to one another as well as to their students, and provide evidence that

> If schools want to enhance their capacity to boost student learning, they should work on building a collaborative culture. . . . When groups, rather than individuals, are seen as the main units for implementing curriculum, instruction, and assessment, they facilitate development of shared purposes for student learning and collective responsibility to achieve it. (Newman & Wehlage, 1995, p. 37)

THE CAPACITY TO GO PUBLIC

Teachers in learning communities eventually learn to go public with their teaching. Such a public stance is in direct contrast to the norms and traditions of what Seymour Sarason (1996) characterized as a "lonely profession." As an occupation, teaching has been long defined by images of the loner who makes a difference in the lives of students through personality, imagination, compassion, discipline, and sheer willpower. From *Good-Bye, Mr. Chips* to *To Sir with Love* to *Stand and Deliver* to *Dangerous Minds*, the media have reinforced the idea that teaching is individualistic, personal, and private and that the good teacher is more often than not at odds with his or her colleagues and has to go it alone. It is clear that professional learning communities challenge this perception; they offer an alternative to the norms of privacy and secrecy and build the capacity of teachers to make their work public.

How does teaching become public? As indicated previously, a powerful vehicle for this transformation is honest talk that focuses on shared texts and problems of practice. The CFGs used protocols that helped teachers focus their attention directly on student work. Group members were given several options about the kinds of work samples they might bring to a session: one piece of work from several students in response to the same assignment, several pieces of work from one student in response to different assignments, one piece of work from a student who completed the assignment successfully, one piece of work from a student who was not able to complete the assignment successfully, work done by students in groups, and visual/audio documentations of students working on or presenting their work (National School Reform Faculty, 1998). Guided by the protocol, the presenting teacher provided the context for the work sample and raised a specific question or concern. Group members asked questions and provided feedback and suggestions. The presenting teacher closed by thinking out loud about how to modify or improve what she had done. The group debriefed. In the Southern Maine Partnership, cross-district groups followed a similar process in looking at and improving assessments that teachers had developed as part of their local assessment systems.

Beyond talk, there was peer observation. Critical Friends Groups developed specific procedures for classroom observations and feedback sessions; each observation was conducted by two colleagues, and feedback occurred within 24 hours. In the Southern Maine Partnership, teams of educators visited one another's schools as part of a School Quality Review process. The observed school raised queries about teaching and learning, and then peer observers visited every classroom, interviewed teachers and students, collected samples of work, and reported findings to the faculty. The roles then reversed: The visitors became the observed, and the observers became the visited.

Before they entered the summer institute, National Writing Project participants were asked to prepare a teaching demonstration and a writing sample that they would be willing to share. In addition, they were expected to produce four written course papers and sit in the "author's chair." Lieberman and Wood (2002) noted

> After a teacher reads a paper aloud from the author's chair, colleagues provide feedback. This feedback, in turn, informs subsequent revisions, and then revisions are also shared. As drafts improve over time, fellows see for themselves how public presentation has the power to motivate and produce high-quality work. (p. 17)

Feedback was in the form of oral or written comments about strengths and suggestions, questions, and reflections about implications for one's own practice. Lieberman and Wood (2002) further reported, "As the ideas and strategies poured out, we saw an ethic of privacy . . . give way to an ethic of 'swapping ideas'" (p. 16).

In the Philadelphia teacher research communities, public sharing took another form. Here teachers constructed oral or written texts that were disseminated internally to group members and externally to a wider audience. These texts included journals, oral inquiries, classroom and school studies, and essays, some of which appear in *Inside/Outside: Teacher Research and Knowledge* (Cochran-Smith & Lytle, 1993).

Perhaps the most innovative example of going public with teaching took place within the CASTL program. The teacher-scholars in the program published images of their practice as exhibitions on a website, which was made available to a wide audience. Each exhibition included a section on context (Where do I teach?), a section on content (What are my students learning?), video clips of classrooms, samples of student work, teacher reflections, resources, and connections to standards. Later, a group of teacher educators was invited to view the website exhibitions and think of ways to use the exhibitions in pre-service teacher preparation. As a result, the teaching practice of the CASTL community has enriched the experience of myriad new teachers. One teacher educator who has used the website in her Adolescent Development classes for three years commented

> along with the multiple images of practice there are multiple images of teachers learning from their practice. Whereas the websites are not constructed to present "best practices," they do provide images of teachers committed to learning in and from their teaching, which leads to better practice all the time. This learning stance towards the work is critically important to the kind of teachers I hope to prepare—and/but it is a stance that I've found is challenging to teach. Because the sites include various forms of teacher reflection (writing, interviews, conversations with colleagues, and so forth) student teachers see veteran teachers actively engaged in their own professional learning. (Richert, 2007)

In Chapter 5, Désirée Pointer Mace describes some of the CASTL exhibitions and their lessons and uses.

THE CAPACITY TO REDEFINE THE TEACHER ROLE

Teachers who are members of learning communities develop the capacity to extend their ideas of what a teacher can do beyond the usual boundaries of the classroom. In the Philadelphia research communities studied by Cochran-Smith and Lytle (1993), the participating teachers became scholars who challenged long held notions of what constitutes research and who is qualified to conduct it. In the CASTL project (Lieberman, 2007), they became public role models for constructing and reflecting on their own instruction. And in the Algebra Group (Little & Horn, 2007), they became curriculum developers and mentors of new teachers.

In a review of the literature, Lieberman and Miller (2004) provide evidence that professional communities support the development of teacher leaders. By their very nature, these cultures where teachers share experience, jointly construct knowledge, and shape common repertoires of practice, provide fertile ground for growing leaders. Examples abound. In some instances leadership development was intentional. In others, leadership emerged from the needs of the community and the talents of its members.

In the National Writing Project (NWP), site directors consciously sought out new leaders and provided them with opportunities to learn to lead. During the summer institutes, the directors "scouted talent" and looked for potential leaders, connected them with others in the larger network, and organized opportunities for them to teach others. By the end of the summer, a cadre of "teacher consultants" had been formed.

> The teacher consultants form a cadre of teacher leaders who work on local, regional, and national levels under the umbrella of the NWP. They are

equipped with theoretical and practical knowledge about how learning takes place; they know the research on literacy development and have the capacity to unpack the research for others; and they have a repertoire of ideas, not a box of recipes. (Lieberman & Miller, 2004, p. 38)

In their home schools and districts, these teacher consultants assumed roles as facilitators of professional development and curriculum leaders. On the national level, they wrote grants and planned collaborative projects. And during the summer institute, they returned as instructors and facilitators. By coupling professional development for improved classroom practice with professional development for leadership, the NWP sites ensured their own vitality and sustainability.

In the Southern Maine Partnership, leadership development was equally intentional in one of its professional communities, the Leadership for Tomorrow's Schools (LTS) project. This project engaged cohorts of teachers in academic and practical work that promoted both improved classroom practice and teacher leadership. In fact, the participants were involved in two professional communities simultaneously: the cross-district community of the LTS cohort and the within-district leadership communities of their home districts. In the first community, members learned from one another about teaching and learning and leading. In the second community, they practiced and performed as teacher leaders and carried out authentic district leadership work. Participants were engaged in tasks such as developing a districtwide induction program, serving as literacy coaches, developing supervision and evaluation models, facilitating assessment development for the district, and contributing to district leadership team meetings. Many LTS participants assumed informal leadership roles after the cohort program was completed, others took on formal teacher-leader positions, while still others moved into administrative leadership ranks.

Elsewhere, leadership development was less intentional, but no less powerful. For example, both the CFGs and the Algebra Group depended on teachers who emerged as facilitative leaders. Little and Horn (2007) report:

Demonstrated patterns of initiative and leadership sustain the group's attention to problems of practice. Building on the record of a former chair who was described as "remarkable at building community," the current co-chairs see themselves as responsible for maintaining the ethos of professional learning in the Algebra Group. They take a visible role in posing questions, eliciting accounts of classroom practice, preserving a focus on teaching and learning— and encouraging initiative of these sorts by others. (np)

But the impact of professional learning communities on the teachers' roles is not limited to movement into leadership roles; it also affected the way classroom teachers experienced teaching. McLaughlin and Talbert (2001) found that teachers who participated in strong-innovative communities enjoyed a greatly enriched teaching career, marked by continuous growth and intrinsic professional rewards. This was not the case in weak or strong-traditional communities. The weak communities tended to enforce norms of privacy and isolation. Their members did not value professional growth and often experienced stagnation and disinterest. In the strong-traditional communities, the situation was different. Here professional growth was valued, but it was viewed solely as a way to earn prestige within the teaching hierarchy. Credentialing led to better teaching assignments. However, while better assignments led to opportunities for more professional growth and for increased rewards for some teachers, it did not do so for all teachers. In the strong-innovative communities, teaching careers took a different turn. Here class assignments were more evenly distributed, equity was privileged over hierarchy, and teachers saw themselves as lifelong learners. They shared their expertise with colleagues, collaborated to improve their practice, and experienced collective—rather than individual—professional rewards and career progress.

3

Balancing Content and Process: Facing Challenges

Ann Lieberman
Lynne Miller

Professional learning communities have two competing agendas that focus on *process* and *content*. There is the push to increase teachers' knowledge of subject matter content and related pedagogies; and there is the necessity of supporting the processes that promote teacher learning and community building. Too much reliance on subject matter may result in a neglect of the means that are necessary to keep a community functional and vital. On the other hand, too much attention to process may result in a neglect of substantive issues and may encourage a move toward generic instructional practices. In these communities while members feel a sense of belonging and enhanced learning, they often fail to make a connection to classroom practice. In both instances, the student experience is not enhanced by teacher membership in professional communities.

Horn (2005) investigated learning communities that were located in the math departments of two high schools with similar demographics: South, with an orientation toward process, and East, home to the Algebra Study Group and with an orientation that combined content and process.

> South's reform program disposed teachers to view problems of schooling through a lens that highlighted the importance of the student–teacher relationships independent of subject considerations, whereas East's math reform framed them in a way that called into question the various relationships among students, teachers, and subject matter. South affiliated with the Coalition of Essential Schools, whereas East's reform was precipitated by a concern for low student engagement in mathematics and fueled by participation in subject-reform networks. (p. 216)

Horn (2005) found that although both groups were engaged in professional learning communities, they were not equally "organized for advancement."
The South teachers did not have time to link whole-school reform to their subject matter and instead, spent their time grappling with such generic issues as
"less is more," a guiding principle of the Coalition of Essential Schools. The
term took on different meanings for different members of the community and,
in the end, proved too vague to catalyze changes in beliefs and practices. As a
result, "the teaching of mathematics at South remained minimally and incon-
sistently transformed by schoolwide, reform efforts" (p. 218).

This was not the case at East, where issues of content and process were
consciously combined. Here the teachers centered their work around the design
of "group worthy" problems, defined as having four characteristics: illustrating
important math concepts, including multiple tasks, allowing for multiple representations, and having several possible solution paths (Horn, 2005). The group
revisited and refined these principles regularly and used them as the "gold stan-
dard" by which they judged their instruction. As a result, the teachers at East
were successful in transforming the math program at the school and succeeded
in engaging a larger proportion of students in high-level math courses.

A major difference between the two groups occurred in what Horn (2005)
referred to as "teaching replays and teaching rehearsals . . . [which are] means
of rendering classroom events in teacher-to-teacher conversation" (p. 225).
At South, the replays and rehearsals took the form of storytelling. Teachers
presented narratives that were edited through their personal lenses and dis-
tanced from teaching mathematics. This form of conversation maintained the
traditional school norm of privacy as teachers censored what they chose to
make public. By contrast, the replays and rehearsals of the teachers at East
drew directly from classroom practice and made frequent use of exemplars of
student work, privileging student voice. They "formed the basis for consulta-
tions, providing evidence through which to reason about practice" (p. 226).

It is clear that in those communities that decoupled process and content, a transformation of teacher practice in the service of enhanced student
learning did not occur. In terms coined by McLaughlin and Talbert (2001),
both South and East exemplified strong communities. However, one was a
strong-traditional community that drew its strength almost exclusively from
the rhetoric of *process*, in this case the process of whole-school reform. The other was a strong professional learning community that relied on the synergy of
content and process, and gave equal attention to subject matter content as well
as to the processes of collegial conversation and lived examples of practice.

While South was an example of a community that maximized process and
minimized content, the social studies department at Oak Ridge High School
(McLaughlin & Talbert, 2001) provided an example of the other extreme, one
that was wedded to "subject matter orthodoxy" (p. 53). At Oak Ridge, teachers bonded around common notions of ascribed student ability and motivation. They stayed committed as a group to traditional texts and materials even
in the face of student disinterest and failure. While *autonomy* at South meant

collective responsibility for student learning, the phrase had a different meaning at Oak Ridge. There, autonomy was synonymous with private and highly personalized practice and served to reinforce conservative and conventional impulses. Transmission teaching was not challenged; student failure was not viewed as a problem of teaching. The department may have functioned as a community, but one that was tied exclusively to subject matter. It had little time to attend to any of the processes associated with collegial discourse, problem posing, and problem solving, and to issues surrounding teacher and student learning. McLaughlin and Talbert (2001) concluded that content-only communities such as this one led to teacher burnout or cynicism.

CHALLENGES COMMUNITIES FACE

As is the case with any new and promising social phenomenon, some proponents of professional learning communities are so invested in the success of the enterprise that they gloss over the inevitable tensions and challenges that arise; they sweep them under the proverbial rug. We are not so disposed. Rather, we believe that by naming tensions inherent in professional learning communities, we can understand them more fully. We have seen challenges emerge in our discussions of context, commitment, capacity, and content. In general, these challenges fall into three categories: navigating fault lines, staying fresh, and dealing with issues of scaling up.

The Challenge of Navigating Fault Lines

Grossman, Wineburg, and Woolworth (2001) introduced the idea of navigating fault lines in their analysis of the Humanities Group. The geological metaphor is apt. In geology, a fault line is defined as a crack or fracture in the earth's crust that is caused by two competing forces that rub against one another. Fault lines may exist side by side for years and millennia, or they may cause enough friction to cause an earthquake. In professional learning communities, fault lines can be characterized as being opposing forces that rub against one another and compete for attention. While most of the time they merely coexist, they always have the potential to explode into full-fledged conflict.

We have uncovered some of the fault lines of professional communities in our previous discussion. These include the fault lines between voluntary and nonvoluntary membership, between community and pseudo-community, between congeniality and collegiality, between process and content, between and across subject matters, between knowledge work and practical work, and between and across group and professional identities. We want to add to this list. As teachers engage in professional learning communities, they often find that they are members of two distinct cultures with two very different sets of norms and values. They have to walk the fault line between the two cultures and meet the challenge of living with the tensions that result (see Table 3.1).

Table 3.1. Negotiating Fault Lines Between Cultures

Norms and Values of Traditional School Cultures	Norms and Values of Professional Learning Communities
Uncertain teaching/learning links	Demonstrations of clear teaching/learning links
Weak, nonconsensual knowledge base	Shared knowledge base
Vague and conflicting goals open to individual interpretation	Announced joint purposes and goals
Competence judged by control of student behavior	Competence judged by demonstrations of student learning
Lack of professional support at induction and throughout the teaching career	Induction of newcomers and continued professional support for veterans
Debate of teaching as art or science	Understanding of teaching as both art and science, mediated by professional judgment
Being private about teaching	Going public with teaching
Valuing practicality, dismissing theory and research	Valuing theory-in-practice, theory-of–practice, and inside/outside knowledge
Simplifying practice, using prescriptions and recipes	Problematizing practice, using inquiry and analysis
Viewing teaching career as flat	Viewing a teaching career as filled with possibilities

Much has been written about the norms and values of schools, those enduring expectations, traditions, practices, beliefs, and habits that mark an institution (Waller, 1967). In an earlier work, we identified what we called "social system understandings" about teaching (Lieberman & Miller, 1992, p. 1). These included: a personalized style forged in isolation from other teachers, a reward system derived primarily from interactions with students and had little or no collegial input, an uncertainty about the links between teaching and learning that leads to constant worry about competence, a weak knowledge base with no consensus about what constitutes good practice, vague and conflicting goals that leads to individual—rather than collective—interpretation and practice, keeping control over students as the major public display of competence, the lack of professional support on entering the profession and throughout the teaching career, and the ongoing debate about the nature of teaching as an art or science.

Central to these social understandings are norms of privacy and practicality. One of the earliest lessons that teachers learn in traditional school cultures is the importance of being private. Privacy is invoked when teachers shy away from sharing experiences, visiting one another's classes, talking about problems of practice, and displaying their successes. Little (1990) described the "persistence of privacy" this way.

> School teaching has endured largely as an assemblage of entrepreneurial individuals whose autonomy is grounded in norms of privacy and noninterference and is sustained by the very organization of teaching work. (p. 530)

Privacy has it advantages. It protects against exposure and censure in cultures that have not developed forums for honest talk.

Practicality also becomes the order of the day. New teachers are rapidly inducted into cultures that view scholarship and research as something that occurs in the ivy tower of universities and has little application to the real life of schools. Being practical means focusing on immediacy and concreteness and leads to the acceptance of teaching scripts, quick fixes, and simple recipes and prescriptions. Being practical is also a survival tactic. It shields teachers from the uncertainly and doubt about one's competence that comes from problematizing practice in a culture where it is considered good form to keep classroom teaching out of view.

While some teachers work in school contexts that have moved beyond these descriptors, such as East High School and Souhegan High School (Horn, 2005; National School Reform Faculty, 1998), most do not. They continue to work in contexts that are more similar to the schools that McLaughlin and Talbert (2001) labeled as weak or strong-traditional cultures. Many of the participants in the Philadelphia research communities and in CASTL taught in such schools, as did the faculty involved in the Humanities Group. For those teachers who straddle two cultures, the fault lines present a special challenge and introduce new fault lines.

Moving back and forth between a traditional school and a professional learning community requires a shift in assumptions, norms, and behaviors. The shift is toward a collective repertoire of teaching practice, a collegial feedback and reward system, an expectation of clear links between teaching and student learning, a shared knowledge base that draws on inside and outside knowledge, publicly announced and collaborative purposes and goals, judgments of teaching competence based on what students can demonstrate about their learning, support for newcomers as well as for veterans in identifying and addressing problems of practice, and a realization that teaching is more art than science and cannot be reduced to simple recipes or prescriptions. These governing norms support collaborative and public work and adhere to Lewin's (1951) idea that "There is nothing so practical as a good theory" (p. 169).

The Challenge of Control

Related to the challenge of two cultures is that of control. Professional learning communities have to figure out how to hold onto control of the content of their agendas in the face of pressure to become what they most eschew: an administrative quick fix to the problems of schooling. Federal, state, and district mandates tend to assume prominence in whole-school professional communities, pushing teacher concerns about practice to the back of the agenda. Training materials and workshops on how to institute professional learning communities (PLCs) are currently offered by diverse professional organizations, such as the South East Education Development Laboratory, the American Association of School Administrators, the Association for Supervision and

Curriculum Development, and the National Staff Development Council. At least one group, Solution Tree, now devotes itself almost exclusively to delivering staff development about how to implement whole-school professional learning communities.

The challenge, then, is to guard against the usurpation of a good idea and to maintain communities that are true to their mission and not viewed as just one more entry into the toolbox of staff development strategies. When communities move from an internal to an external locus of control, they dilute their power as transformative forums for teaching and learning. Diane Wood (2007) explains the challenge this way:

> On the one hand, there is the charge for teachers to take ownership over their own work and development through LC work; on the other, there is the message that administrators, finally, control the content of the meetings. Although teachers and administrators ought to share the same work, working together so that all students learn, the hierarchical nature of most school cultures frequently means that administrators define and direct that work and teachers become socialized to that reality. (p. 732)

She concludes that in losing control of their agendas, members of teaching communities may find themselves replacing norms of collective autonomy for norms of compliance.

The other challenge to control is in the area of process and can be stated as "Who controls the conversation?" At one end of the continuum of control are the Algebra Study Group and the math department at East High School, where leaders emerge from within the group and from within the context of strong, collaborative department cultures. At the other end is the Humanities Group, in which the authors were, by their own description, viewed as both project organizers and leaders. In the first two cases community thrived; in the third, it did not.

There is also some question about the role of protocols in professional communities. Designed as an aid to collegial conversation, they have proven effective in focusing attention on student work and teacher practice, offering opportunities for equal participation, and adding to the productivity of group talk (Little & Curry, 2008; Wood, 2007) as demonstrated in the video vignette of the CFG at Souhegan High School. But, protocols also have the potential in less developed contexts to "develop a certain formulaic or ritual character in which form takes precedence over substance" and to fail to acknowledge the fault lines that exist between and among subject matters (Little & Curry, 2008, np). The protocols require trained facilitators to make choices about what protocols to use. This may leave group members out of decision making about which processes will guide conversation and exacerbate tensions surrounding control of processes.

The Challenge of Scaling Up

In six of our cases the work of the communities remained fairly local. The Southern Maine Partnership and the National Writing Project are the two exceptions. Each engaged in efforts to scale up their organizations and, in so doing, had to confront a new set of challenges that took the form of a threat of mission drift, the temptation to control process, the appeal of accommodating external demands, and the lure of centralizing authority and leadership. Each organization took a different path, and each met with a different result that had major implications for the contexts they provided for the development and sustainability under their umbrellas.

The Southern Maine Partnership began in 1985 when six district superintendents, an education dean, and a college professor came together to figure out how a university and its neighboring schools could find common ground and help one another improve student success and enhance professional learning in the region. What began as a small network grew unexpectedly and exponentially. Expanding to over 30 member districts, it had to face the challenge of growing to meet the needs of the region and staying tied to its roots as a regional, boundary-crossing collaborative where collegial conversation about member-generated agendas sustained multiple and diverse professional learning communities.

The Partnership was successful in preserving its regional nature. Even though more districts had joined, the organization was still bounded by geography. Educators from diverse institutions were able to travel to a common site and form multiple and diverse learning communities. The ability to maintain regionalism in the midst of growth kept the Partnership honest and focused it on the issues that mattered most to its members. Miller (2001) explained

> Because a partnership is a regional entity, it struggles to maintain a local agenda within a state policy environment. It must respond to state initiatives, of course, but it must also remain true to grassroots interests and priorities. A partnership must also guard against being unduly influenced by external funding agents and national affiliations. Its power derives from its ability to remain connected to local concerns, issues, talents, and capabilities. (p. 116)

The Partnership's capacity to cross boundaries was enhanced rather than hindered by its expansion. It retained its identity as an organization that was neither fish nor fowl, neither university nor school. Because it stood outside of both institutions, it could make its own rules about how to accommodate new members and increase its effectiveness as an incubator for growing professional communities.

> Bridging two cultures, it remains marginal to each. This marginality, though difficult to manage, is essential for survival. It now only protects against over-identification with one institution; it guarantees that diverse and multiple voices will be heard and valued. (Miller, 2001, p. 116)

This stance allowed the Partnership to become a safe place for an increasing number of regional educators to engage in honest conversation and play with ideas without feeling the need to champion or implement them. At one point, over 17 school–university learning communities met regularly over dinner. Reciprocal dialogue was the "coin of the realm" with little tolerance for didacticism or prescriptions about practice.

Maintaining a lean staff in the face of expansion was essential in protecting the Partnership as a member-driven organization. Conversation was horizontal and not vertical; leadership was embedded in the professional communities as they developed and was not administered by outside authorities. The flow of the organization, from the periphery to the center, was synonymous with the flow of learning that took place. Reciprocal interactions were the major catalysts for learning.

Throughout the scaling up from 6 to over 30 member districts, the Partnership paid due diligence to maintaining its core mission and values. However, a second opportunity to expand did not fare so well. The change was gradual but dramatic. The Partnership received a very large subcontract from a grant that was officially housed in another organization. New staff were hired and set about the task of helping high schools reflect on and redesign their curriculum and teaching to reach a broader span of students. The original plan of the grant was to engage with a small number of schools to develop understandings about the process that could help Partnership members and other educators in their own local efforts. But the official grantees had different ideas. They quickly urged the adoption of an expanded mandate that had explicit products and outcomes. As the grant took on a life of its own, going wider became more valued than going deeper. Staff allegiance to the region waned. School–university collaboration was minimized and, in fact, eliminated. Professional communities still existed, but in smaller number and with less organizational support. Formal meetings that had preset agendas and facilitator-structured discussions were introduced. As the public profile of the grant's work increased, that of the Partnership diminished. Halfway through the funding cycle, it became obvious that in its second attempt to scale up, the Partnership had lost its way. The due diligence that had been paid in the past to maintaining its signature characteristics had not been sustained. The result was a drifting away from mission, values, and practices. Only by separating itself from the grant could the Partnership begin to recapture its identity and reclaim its capacity to generate and sustain true professional learning communities, which had ebbed and flowed with the fluctuations in the organization.

The scaling-up experience of the National Writing Project (NWP) stands in marked contrast to that of the Southern Maine Partnership. It began in 1974 as a regional collaborative in the San Francisco Bay Area and expanded to include over 195 sites in all 50 states, Washington, D.C., and Puerto Rico, and to involve over 2 million teachers and administrators (Lieberman & Wood, 2002). What allowed the organization to scale up to such an extent and not lose its way? It seems that there are two vital elements: *leadership* and *social and core practices* that paid due diligence to maintaining the NWP's mission, values, and practices.

The leadership of the NWP, both at the central office and in the sites, maintained a commitment to grassroots democracy and the belief that teachers' experiences were worthy of being valued and disseminated. By avoiding the trap of becoming experts, leaders enacted the principles of teacher empowerment that they espoused. Site leaders

> attended and participated in the institute, benefiting from experiential learning in the same way as other participants. They were at different times teacher, facilitator, broker, fund-raiser, entrepreneur, decision maker, proposal writer, organizer—and, most important, "cultural carrier" of the Writing Project way of working. (Lieberman & Wood, 2002, p. 48)

And the NWP leaders made sure to distribute leadership widely by providing opportunities for participants to become teacher consultants and leaders in their own right.

The *social practices* of the NWP, though not explicitly articulated, were embedded in all aspects of its work (Lieberman & Wood, 2002). These are: valuing each member, honoring teacher knowledge, creating forums for sharing, investing learners with leadership, drawing on practice and relationships, providing multiple entry points, engaging in reflection, sharing leadership, promoting inquiry, and encouraging identity as member of a community.

Finally, *core practices* remained consistent in all sites. These included practices that engaged all participants in writing and making their writing public, demonstrating their teaching to one another and providing feedback, and reading educational research and conducting inquiry. In addition, having food at all meetings, ensuring a comfortable and welcoming space, and celebrating success were all traditions that extended across NWP sites.

While most professional communities do not make the decision to scale up, they can learn from the histories of those who did. This is especially true as professional learning communities prepare to face the emerging challenge to teacher power over their own learning.

PULLING IT ALL TOGETHER

Our goal in writing this chapter was to build understandings about professional learning communities, unravel some of the complexities about what they are, and articulate their signature theories and practices. Our approach was unorthodox. Instead of doing a traditional review of the literature, we chose to focus on eight cases from the research and from our own experience. And rather than reporting on each case separately, we opted to tie them together under the umbrella of five big ideas or themes: context, commitment, capacity, content, and challenges. What did we find?

- *Context matters.* Factors such as where a community is located, the culture that surrounds it, the way it gets started, and its conditions of membership combine to impact the trajectories it takes and the challenges it faces.
- *Commitments take time to develop.* There is no such thing as an instant community. Members have to get to know one another and build norms of trust before they can commit to the process of learning from one another. As members reach agreement about how to talk, think, and view their collective work, they develop identification with the group; commitments deepen. When this happens successfully, it does so over time and along an uncharted path.
- *Capacity of members to engage fully in teaching communities grows as commitments develop.* They learn how to talk together honestly, to engage in knowledge work both as producers and critical consumers of new theories and ideas, and to make connections among their own learning, their teaching practices, and the impact these have on students. Members also develop the capacity to act in ways that often run counter to the cultural norms of their schools. They learn to go public with their teaching, opening themselves to collegial scrutiny, feedback, critique, and taking advantage of the opportunity to display their successes and to influence others. And they begin to see themselves and act differently. They reinvent themselves as teachers, reinvigorate their careers, and, in many instances, assume positions of leadership in matters of teaching and learning.
- *Content matters, but is has to be balanced with process.* Communities grapple with the problem of how to attend to the need to deepen subject matter knowledge and content-related pedagogies and, at the same time, concentrate on the processes that make the community alive and strong. While it is impossible to keep the balance all of the time, communities need to guard against going too far in either direction.
- *Challenges are endemic to any ambitious social enterprise,* and professional learning communities are no exception. Chief among the challenges is navigating the fault line between membership in a learning community, with its collectively developed norms, values, and ways of doing business, and membership in schools and districts that often have a very different ways of operating. Community members need to help one another develop strategies for straddling both worlds. They also have to address the challenges to autonomy that present when external policies and mandates impose on the agenda of the group and when decisions about processes within the group are not collectively made. Finally, there is the challenge that some communities face when they decide to move beyond their initial boundaries and scale up. Here, as in all other challenges, it is important to revisit goals and mission and to maintain working relationships and agreed-upon social practices.

PART II

Learning from Practice and Reflection

The five cases presented in this section were written by project directors who were very much engaged in the practical work of teaching communities. Taken together, the cases demonstrate how people in a variety of settings create and sustain collaborative cultures where teachers are able to develop new capacities and new competencies within a community of peers. The cases describe how each venture developed, and they detail the hopes the project directors brought to the work, what they envisioned teachers would learn, and how they thought teachers would learn it. The five directors made the development of both teaching competence and professional community central to their work; they found that realizing this goal was sometimes challenging, sometimes energizing, and sometimes painless.

The narratives are thick with detail and complexity. In Chapter 9, we seek to synthesize the cases, to cull generalizations that are useful and important, and to articulate the common ground where getting better (whatever the content) and working within a teaching community exist side by side. We begin by introducing the cases, and then discuss them in relation to the five themes that frame this volume: context, capacity, content, commitment, and challenge.

INTRODUCING THE CASES

Christine Cziko writes in Chapter 4 about her students who are studying to be teachers in the Multicultural Urban Secondary English (MUSE) program at the University of California at Berkeley. Her story describes the tension between a teacher educator's quest to give students a conceptual and practical way of thinking about practice and the students' expressed needs for "survival tools." Navigating this fault line, Cziko develops a community of inquiring teachers.

Désirée H. Pointer Mace describes three different groups who go public with their teaching, learning, and collaboration. In Chapter 5, she extends the idea of community to include a network of people joined together through the discussion, examination, and use of one another's multimedia websites. Three teachers in three different contexts provide models of competence through their websites, and virtual communities develop around them.

In Chapter 6, Ellen Moir, founder and director of the New Teacher Center at University of California–Santa Cruz, tells the story of how she and her colleagues came to realize that those who were mentoring new teachers needed a community of their own so that they could improve their practice. The narrative of the development of the Mentor Forum is about helping mentors go public with their problems as a way of building community and enhancing their mentoring skills, abilities, and knowledge.

In Chapter 7, Matt Ellinger describes his and Liping Ma's work with an elementary school for 2 years. He describes the change in the patterns of communication, colleagueship, motivation, and changed identity as teachers deepened and broadened their knowledge of mathematics and learned how to teach it well.

Mayumi Shinohara and Kirsten Daehler describe a science program in Chapter 8 that is designed to help teachers deepen their science learning. The challenge of creating a community of learners and facilitating the understanding of science proves to be necessary, yet problematic. The chapter describes why these ideas are often in tension and how the codirectors struggled with these seemingly compatible, yet different objectives.

4

Meeting at the Cafe to Do Teacherly Things: Community and Competence in a Teacher Preparation Program

Christine Cziko

How does a person learn to be a teacher? This is the question I have been asking myself for the past 10 years. I have had plenty of experience teaching. I taught English Language Arts for 25 years in urban middle and high schools. I spent 20 of those years in underperforming schools in the Bronx, New York, and the rest in what was described as a "tough" neighborhood in San Francisco. I helped to start two new schools and I have been a teacher consultant for both the New York City Writing Project and the Bay Area Writing Project.

THE CREATION OF THE "MUSE" PROGRAM

In 1997 I was hired by the Graduate School of Education to help start an English Credential/MA program at UC Berkeley. This program was to be called the Multicultural Urban Secondary English (MUSE) Credential and MA Program. The goal of MUSE is to prepare the best possible English teachers for the schools that need them most. Since the bulk of my own teaching experience had been in urban settings, I thought it was a job that I could do.

I knew that one of my hardest tasks would be to make explicit to both myself and my students the factors that influenced my teaching decisions. These decisions were internalized and made very rapidly in the classroom, and now I would have to unpack the theories that were underlying both my planning and my actual teaching. It wasn't just about what I did—but about *why* I did it. The ability to plan and teach based on sound pedagogical theory is particularly necessary for new teachers who want to teach in urban settings where resources are often scarce and students are often struggling.

In the literature, information sessions, and admission interviews for the MUSE program, we made it clear that we had a specific mission. This was a program for future urban schoolteachers who were committed to meeting the needs of all students. Although it was a small program, our candidates were highly accomplished in their own prior academic work, and most had experience with urban adolescents in some kind of learning environment.

CONTEXT

MUSE is a 1½-year Credential/MA program. During the first year, students take two graduate courses in the summer. The following fall, they begin with a 1-week intensive writing workshop and then move into a program that consists of 20 hours of student teaching per week and four graduate courses. In the spring, they continue with their student teaching requirement and take three graduate courses. By June of that first year, they receive their credential.

In the second year of the program, students find their own teaching jobs and meet every other week in groups of no more than 10, which are led by a faculty MA advisor. During this year, the new teachers pick an education-related question that concerns them—usually involving their own students, classes, schools, or communities—and undertake a teacher research project. They decide upon a question, collect data, analyze what they have collected, draw conclusions, and sometimes make recommendations. Finally, they write up their research project, which must be approved by two faculty members. This research project is the final requirement of their master's degree, which they receive in May of their second year.

When I started directing and teaching in the MUSE program, I thought about all the things I had learned over my 25 years of teaching. What was crucial for me to teach my students? What was the best way for them to learn? What could only be learned over time in their own classroom? Were there things about teaching that couldn't be taught? What did I learn from others? I thought little, if at all about building a learning community within the MUSE program. I knew that, in the past, when I was able to achieve a sense of community in my own middle and high school classes, we could all do more and learn more. Students helped each other, there was no ridicule or fear of failure, and we shared a sense of purpose. I wasn't always successful in building this kind of community—students had to trust me and one another—but when it did happen it was magical.

Thinking back, although I knew the value of community and how it led to competence in one setting, I didn't make the transition to the setting of my pre-service teachers. After all, they had so much to learn in so little time. I did think that being in graduate classes together and sharing their student teaching experiences would lead to some kind of community, but I assumed that would just be icing on the cake. We didn't have time for extras, and I had so much to teach them. In retrospect I now realize that, since teaching can be an isolated job and yet also a job in which one feels extremely vulnerable, a supportive community was essential.

HOW MY THINKING CHANGED

From the start, I chose three learning principles that I believed would be at the heart of the program: apprenticeship, inquiry, and collaboration. I'd worked with these ideas for many years—both in my classroom and in professional groups that I belonged to, including the National Writing Project. I discussed these principles with my students beginning at orientation, but they had different ideas about what they needed. Inquiry bit the dust first. Students wanted me to *tell* them how to teach—that's what they were in the program for—not to discover it for themselves. They wanted a foundation of sound theory and effective practice. They argued that they had an entire career to engage in inquiry.

Collaboration was the next victim. They shared plenty of trials and tribulations, and some triumphs, from their classrooms, but there was little collective problem solving, at least initially. They planned independently for their classes under the guidance of a cooperating teacher, and they essentially felt alone standing in front of the class. Only if they were in a collaborative school setting, where teachers planned together, would they actually experience collaboration. In urban schools, these settings were hard to come by.

And so, in the end it was apprenticeship that ruled. Their cooperating teachers modeled teaching in their own classes while student teachers watched and imitated. I modeled teaching techniques in the methods class and my students watched and imitated what I did. My first big learning experience was recognizing the tension between the novice teacher's need to know concretely what to do on Monday and the teacher educator's quest to learn conceptually and practically how to teach these future teachers.

It took me 3 or 4 years to start thinking seriously about community in the MUSE program. I somehow got the idea that if the students became competent teachers, they would naturally form communities of like-minded teachers. But students weren't going to become competent teachers in a 1-year program. And without trust in the group, their willingness to take risks or admit failure was going to hold them back from learning to teach. I began to think that community might come first and that it could lead to competence, rather than the other way around. I decided to plan a specific series of activities that would support the building of a MUSE community. My hope was that this would build the kind of trust necessary for students to be open to learning about teaching.

THE BUILDING BLOCKS:
ORIENTATION AND SHARED COMMUNITY EVENTS

The program officially begins with an orientation at my home 1 or 2 days be-fore classes start in June. Luckily, the Bay Area summer is predictable enough to allow students to use both indoor and outdoor space. I provide the food, and while we talk, eat, and meet, you can feel students' anxiety levels fall. I invite MUSE supervisors, alumni, faculty, and student services personnel. Not every one of these people comes, but there are always some, and I think the students are reassured that they will be well taken care of. I was surprised to learn that having this event in my home is significant for many of the stu-dents. They send me e-mails over the following few days thanking me for "opening my house" to them. It isn't something they expect.

LEARNING ABOUT ONE ANOTHER

After giving the students an overview of the summer and providing them with the information that they need and some time to ask questions, we do a sharing activity. Everyone introduces him- or herself and tells a short story about his or her name. Students talk about where their names come from and how they feel about their names, and they share funny and sad stories. Over the years, we have had Asian American students named after Johnny Carson and Loretta Young. We had a student whose name, unfortunately, is the same as a major restroom paper supply company. We've even had a Steve Martin in the group. Students tell stories of being named after grandparents, of their mixed race backgrounds, and of how their name was a way to keep family memories alive. A Vietnamese student's name meant "far from Vietnam." A Latina woman was named after her father's favorite Mexican actress, who unfortunately made a career change and became a porn star. I was called Christine Psycho (instead of Cziko) all through high school after a nun mispronounced my name during the first week of class and it stuck. It always amazes me how this simple activity can yield such rich stories. It also becomes a demonstration of the diversity we have in our group—diversity that is not always obvious from just looking at one another. This is our first important learning activity. As teachers, in order to help our students become successful we have to create a safe space for them to tell their stories, we have to listen to those stories carefully, and then we must build on what we learn from each student.

LEARNING ABOUT THE COMMUNITY

In addition to their graduate class work, we follow up the orientation with a "Community Events" assignment. I want to give students a way to connect with and learn about the communities in which they are going to be teaching as well as to help them continue to learn about one another. Students are required to attend three community events with at least two other MUSE students and to write a report on the experience. Getting students to see one another outside of class and in locations outside of their comfort zone forces them to rely more upon one another.

Students often go on the Mission Mural tour, explore community gardens, attend Oakland poetry slams, and visit community centers set up to support gay and lesbian youth. Some students with knowledge of the neighborhoods organize guided trips. Over and over, students report that they had "never done anything like this before" or had "never gone to a place like this before." Many admit that without their fellow MUSE students to accompany them, they would never have had such diverse experiences. In this way they are already learning to take chances and to trust their colleagues.

LEARNING TO BE A WRITER

MUSE students return to campus 1 week before regular classes begin. We use this week for a writing workshop. In my 25 years as an NWP teacher consultant, I have learned how important writing can be in building community. I know it is important for MUSE students to experience the power of writing for themselves and hope they will commit to making writing a central focus in their future classrooms.

UNLOCKING THE IDEAS FOR WRITING

We start this workshop with a generating activity called the "Memory Chain." This is one of many activities I learned in the NWP to help students come up with a topic they want to write about. In this activity, you start by writing down a memory or a brief phrase or sentence and then continue to add more memories that connect to the previous one. A sample would be: "I remember my grandmother's pies, which remind me of being at her house for the summer, which reminds me of missing my parents, which reminds me of being punished when I got caught smoking, which reminds me. . . ." Students write for 10 to 15 minutes or until they have at least a page of memories from which they can choose a topic. These memories are funny, sad, painful, and soothing and often deal with topics students have never written about before.

Working through the process of draft, writing groups, revision, writing groups, final copy, editing groups, and a public read-around never fails to bring students together as a community of writers and future teachers. The read-around is particularly moving, with the reader cheered on and supported by his or her writing group. On occasion, a student takes it upon herself to collect the pieces and create an e-anthology of everyone's work. On the end-of-year evaluation, there are always some students who write that this week of writing and sharing was the most powerful part of the program for them.

Simultaneously, students prepare to meet their cooperating teachers. Each student writes a letter introducing him- or herself to his or her cooperating teacher; explaining why he or she wants to teach; sharing his or her personal background, experiences, and strengths; and finally stating what he or she wants to learn from the cooperating teacher. The students thank their cooperating teachers for opening up their classrooms and agreeing to mentor them. This is the first step in entering the community of the school site. I have heard from numerous cooperating teachers how important this letter is to them and how it makes the process of getting to know one another that much easier. In this letter, once again the students are taking risks and sharing their personal lives with someone they don't know. Writing a letter is a small thing, but it is the start of an important mentoring relationship.

STUDENT-INITIATED SOCIAL AND ACADEMIC ACTIVITIES

As students begin the hectic schedule of student teaching and taking graduate courses, they already have a solid foundation of friendship and respect for one another. This encourages ongoing social and academic activities. Whole group and small group activities are constantly being organized by the students. One student was so excited about getting her first set of class papers to grade that she e-mailed everyone to ask if anyone wanted to meet in the local cafe to do "teacherly" things with her. A small group of students showed up on a Saturday morning. In fact, one student told me that the local cafe should make a contribution to the program. The MUSE students spent many hours teaching and learning from each other over dozens of cups of coffee. Sometimes their get togethers were purely social. From housewarmings to spoken word performances, from baby showers to birthday parties—being together strengthened the bonds of this deepening community.

EXPANDING THE FOCUS OF INTELLECTUAL ACTIVITY

Each year, smaller groups of students get together for specific purposes. Study groups among college students are, of course, common, and MUSE students do form study groups around different graduate classes, but there are almost always students who get together for reading and writing. Book groups are popular, with a focus on adolescent literature. Each group member reads a different book and then gives a presentation to the whole group on both the content of the book and teaching ideas for the book. With new, quality adolescent books coming out each year, it is impossible for one teacher alone to keep up. Some students continue with the writing workshop experience despite the effort and diligence needed to keep writing.

CELEBRATING OUR LEARNING

Before the winter break, the MUSE students again meet at my home for a potluck meal in celebration of the end of the semester. After eating (always a top priority), the students write. On one side of an index card, they write one thing they learned about themselves as learners. On the other side, they write one thing they want to make sure they learn in the second semester. Each student reads what he or she has written aloud. As Lee Shulman (1986) says, "Teaching is the learning profession." Having future teachers focus on themselves as learners is the key to the program. They will continue to learn throughout their teaching careers, but there are specific things—skills, processes, understandings—that the program can provide for them and, in this activity we ask them what these things are. Since I have the luxury of teaching them for a whole year, I can revise parts of my spring syllabus to include the issues raised by my students. These issues often include: responding to student writing, leading class discussions, effectively working with groups of students, and, without fail, classroom management.

We end by distributing a "MUSE Care Package" to each student, which consists of a brown paper lunch bag containing survival tools for next semester:

MUSE Care Package

Gum—to remind you to "stick with it"
Rubber bands—to remind you to stay flexible
Snickers—to remind you to take time out to laugh
Lifesavers—to remind you what you might be for a student one day
Chocolate kisses—to remind you that someone loves you
Smarties—to help you on days your brain doesn't want to
Peanuts—to remind you that all great teachers are a little crazy
Tootsie Rolls—to remind you not to bite off more than you can chew
Butterfingers—to remind you that everyone drops the ball sometime
Paper bag —to help you keep it together and give you food for thought!

Amid much laughter, students leave for a well-earned holiday. Each year, they appear to have learned a lot about the importance of context. Who are my students? What do they need? How can I be the best teacher possible for them? And each year I relearn how complex the act of teaching is and how lucky I am to work with these dedicated young people who want to make a difference in their students' lives.

A TIME OF TRANSITION

When students return from winter break, they are placed with a new cooperating teacher in a new student teaching assignment. They also take different graduate classes except for the yearlong methods course that I teach. This is definitely a time of transition. They miss their students from last semester, no matter how much they may have struggled with and complained about them, and they have to get used to a whole different school setting. Some students go to alternative schools, others teach English as a Second Language (ESL), and many move from middle school to high school or visa versa.

GAINING SUPPORT THROUGH PROFESSIONAL ORGANIZATIONS

Again, students rely on one another for support. When possible we put more than one student teacher at the same site, each with a cooperating teacher. More frequently we are able to place our student teachers with cooperating teachers who are MUSE alumni. MUSE alumni want to do the best job possible for their student teachers as well as for the program. They clearly remember what worked and what didn't in their own student teaching experience. When placed with a MUSE alum, the student teacher often feels that he or she has an ally who speaks the same language and shares the same beliefs about teaching and learning. Of course, this is not always true, but pairings with MUSE alumni usually work out well.

Students have another assignment that helps them think about which communities they may want to enter after they have their credential. All students have to take part in at least two professional development activities outside of their own school site. As with the community event assignment, students have to write up their experiences and share them with the rest of the class. I urge them to attend a professional development activity sponsored by an educational organization. Students have attended workshops sponsored by the Bay Area Writing Project, Teachers for Social Justice, Facing History and Ourselves, California Association of Teachers of English, and education programs connected to theaters, museums, and libraries. We discuss the importance of being part of a professional community outside of one's school site and the resources these communities provide. I also urge students to go to activities together and pool the knowledge they gain.

VISITING AND VIDEOTAPING

MUSE students must complete the Performance Assessment for California Teachers (PACT) to receive their credential. This final requirement is an intensive examination of their planning, teaching, assessment, and reflection on a

3- to 5-hour teaching event in their student teaching assignment. It is part of their lead teaching requirement. (For a complete description of PACT go to http://www.pacttpa.org)

One of the PACT requirements is that the student teacher be videotaped, and 10 minutes of uncut teaching must be included in the PACT final product. Even the most experienced teacher is more self-conscious when being observed. Being filmed for a high-stakes assessment is that much harder. I encourage students to volunteer to videotape for their classmates. They often discuss the lesson and collaborate on what the focus of the video should be. Many students have told me that it made a big difference to have a fellow student tape them, not only because they were both going through the experience of being videotaped, but also because they trusted each other. The student being videotaped knew that his or her partner's goal was to show the best teaching that was going on in the room.

In addition to videotaping, we encourage student teachers to visit other sites in order to get a sense of the kind of school they want to teach in. As they begin their job search, many are drawn to schools where other MUSE students are teaching. In March, I start getting e-mails from MUSE alumni telling me that there will be openings in their schools and asking if I can spread the word to my current MUSE students. Even more heartening are the messages I get from administrators—principals and department heads who have hired MUSE students in the past and are eager to hire more. At least half of the English departments in four Bay Area schools are made up of MUSE alumni. Many other schools have two to five MUSE alumni working in their English departments. MUSE graduates are forming their own community clusters in many of the places where they are hired. In the 10 years that the MUSE program has been in existence, not one of our approximately 220 graduates was unable to find a teaching position. Although some graduates have decided to return to the university to get their PhD or attend law school or medical school, the numbers are insignificant.

FROM STUDENT TEACHER TO TEACHER

For the last time, students gather at my home at the end of the spring semester. Many have jobs lined up, others are still searching, but no one is panicked. Everyone is ready for a summer break. After informal talking, eating, and laughing, students sit in a circle and talk in turn about the most important things they have learned this year. Some of these things have nothing to do with me or the program. Often they talk about what they've learned about themselves—that yes, they do have a teacher voice that they just had to set free, or that they have developed eyes in the back of their head, or, more seriously, that they didn't know they could feel so passionately about young people who were so different than themselves.

This is when we take out our gift to each student—a Doctor Seuss book titled *Hooray for Diffendoofer Day*. It is the story of a very unusual school where students learn to "teach frogs to dance and pigs to put on underpants." One day the principal announces that every school in the area must take a test. If the students do not pass, the school will be destroyed. But the teachers are confident. The popular Miss Bonkers assures the students that they've learned the most important skill of all: to think. As students take turns reading each page aloud the hilarity builds until they reach the predictably successful ending and everyone cheers.

But we end our last gathering on a more serious note. They all know that things are much simpler in the world of Doctor Seuss than in the real world. Even though I often remind them that they can only be "the best first-year teacher you can be," they know they will need all the support and help they can get in the coming years. This is when I bring out the lanyards—the universal symbol of K–12 teachers.

We all stand in a circle and I hand each student a lanyard telling him or her to just hold on to it. We then have the "teacher version" of an MA hooding ceremony in recognition of the hard work they have done to become certified and, in time, excellent teachers. Each student walks up to another and puts the lanyard over that student's head. A hug usually follows. I find this one of the most moving experiences in the program. I can just see them stepping up, moving from student teacher to teacher. I can see them relying on one another, sharing their strengths and asking for help when they are in trouble. Their learning continues as their community supports them, allowing them to take risks and continue to celebrate their accomplishments.

5

Learning from Practice/ Learning in Practice: Using Multimedia to Support Teacher Development

Désirée H. Pointer Mace

The professional lives of accomplished teachers don't begin at 8:00 A.M. and end at 3:00 P.M. Neither are they limited to the four walls of their classrooms. Many veteran K–12 teachers are also experienced leaders (Lieberman & Miller, 2004). They work as teacher educators, authors of curriculum, and professional developers. They develop informal afterschool workshops and seminars, provide guidance to new teachers in mentorship programs, assume roles of leadership in national curriculum or reform networks, or work as faculty in teacher education programs. But most of this work that they do is invisible. Their accomplishments and effectiveness are often measured solely by their students' achievement on standardized tests. To be sure, student outcomes are a vital measure of teachers' work and professional accomplishments. But they are not the only measure.

Even when teachers gather together, there are few opportunities for them to center their professional learning on practice—their own or others'. Teacher-leaders may bring in pieces of student work to prompt discussion or form video clubs (Sherin, 2004), but only rarely have these engaging artifacts of practice been preserved and made public so that others might use them for professional learning. However, the terrain is now shifting; innovative multimedia records of practice are being put online, shedding light on teachers' questions, challenges, and collaborations. Teacher educators are beginning to use these websites as alternative texts in their courses and programs. Communities of professional learning, similarly, can become engaged in making their practice public, learning from the practice of others, and sharing their methods for interrogating practice with other teacher learning communities.

The advent of multimedia helps us shine light on all these different domains of professional practice and show their interconnections, affording us opportunities to reflect on teaching in all its complexity, and making public the intricacies of accomplished practice. If we follow an accomplished teacher throughout the many domains of her professional life, what can this teach us about the profession as a whole? This chapter describes how teachers at different stages in their careers have created records of practice that can be applied to different spheres of teacher learning. By doing so, a continuum of professional development can be made visible, and the communities in which teachers learn can extend beyond the walls of their schools.

Three different examples of K–12 teachers' practice illustrate how, why, and to what ends practitioners go public with their teaching, their learning, and their collaborations and reveal what they learn from doing so and what they teach others. Yvonne Hutchinson, a 39-year veteran teacher, is able to share the expertise accrued over decades in the classroom; Phil Levien, in a sheltered English and special needs setting, reinterprets the art of Shakespeare for a diverse school community; and Jennifer Myers shows how a novice teacher adapts and enacts curriculum drawn from her professional development experiences.

Hutchinson, Levien, and Myers teach in three different contexts with very different student populations. Their multimedia records of teaching practice provide us with three different models for developing and demonstrating competence and for enacting and sustaining community in a teaching life. Because all three of these teachers have made parts of their teaching lives public, they have expanded the scope of competence and community beyond the walls of their own classrooms, raising new questions about whose competence is developing and which communities are being affected by their teaching innovations. Their websites provide a rare opportunity to see that the creation of a multimedia record of practice not only connects the authoring teachers to a global community of likeminded scholars, but also allows the teachers to represent the intrinsically multilayered nature of teaching work through the use of nonlinear hypertext tools.

LEARNING FROM AND WITH
THE PRACTICE OF YVONNE DIVANS HUTCHINSON

Yvonne Divans Hutchinson is a National Board Certified Teacher who has taught Secondary English in Los Angeles for nearly 40 years. In that time, Hutchinson has developed many accomplished practices, both within her classroom and beyond. Within the classroom, she has developed a curriculum that encourages every student to participate in rigorous discussions of literary texts, bridges her African American and Hispanic students' facilities with oral expression by offering them opportunities to express themselves in written narratives, and integrates canonical and alternative texts within a social justice framework that encourages students to develop their confidence as public intellectuals.

Particularly after her certification as a National Board teacher, Hutchinson was asked repeatedly to provide videos of her classroom teaching or to open up her room to visitors and observers. In part to address these requests, Hutchison developed a website about her classroom practice as part of her fellowship in the Carnegie Academy for the Scholarship of Teaching and Learning (CASTL).[1]

Hutchinson's website focuses largely on one instructional day in her 9th-grade English class at King-Drew Medical Magnet School[2] when she facilitated a discussion of jazz musician Willie Ruff's (1991) memoir *A Call to Assembly*. On the morning when Hutchison and her students discussed the text, the students had completed an "anticipation guide"[3] that asked them to take a position regarding some polarizing statements about the text, such as "A person should always follow the phrase 'Honor thy father and mother,' even if he or she thinks that his or her mother and father are wrong."

In the selection the students had read prior to this day, Ruff describes his first experiences hearing "the N word." He had gotten his first job, and another employee at the small shop where he was hired was deaf. Ruff, already intoxicated by the communicative potential of music and sound, was fascinated by the sign language used between employer and employee, and implored his (White) employer to teach him to sign. As the employer teaches him a particular sign, he tells Ruff to "raise your fist like you're going to hit a nigger." Ruff is stunned by this use of the word and leaves work vowing never to return. When he gets home, his grandmother tells him that his employer had called and complained that Ruff was rude to him. Ruff explains to her what happened, and she responds that his boss wasn't saying it to him and tells him to go back to work and "stoop to conquer." When Ruff gets back to work, he sees that his employer is smug about his return. Ruff realizes that he cannot stoop to conquer, and instead of saying "I quit!" to his employer, he signs it to him and then leaves for good.[4]

On her website, Hutchinson's students articulately and passionately describe their responses to the text and the connections they made to their own personal lives. Throughout, Hutchinson intervenes periodically to guide the students back to the text, to encourage a reticent student to participate, and to direct the students into or out of particular discussion configurations. The website includes an hour-long reflective interview[5] with Hutchinson about her personal, pedagogical, and curricular priorities for her classroom, as well as an afterschool conversation between Hutchinson and four of her students about her high expectations for them and the nature of the work she expects them to engage in during the class.

Hutchinson's website has been used as an alternative "text" in many different teacher education settings. Pam Grossman, Professor of Curriculum and Instruction in English at Stanford University, has used Hutchinson's work to drive an assignment about the facilitation of discussions around literary texts in secondary English classrooms.[6] Kathy Schultz at the University of Pennsylvania has incorporated Hutchinson's "class scribe" activity into her own teaching methods in a course on Reading and Writing in the Elementary Classroom.[7] Anna Richert of Mills College considers Hutchinson a "silent teaching partner" in her course on Adolescent Development,[8] and Gloria Ladson-Billings of the University of Wisconsin at Madison has used Hutchinson as an example of "teaching controversial subjects" in a course on Social Studies Methods.

Similarly, Hutchinson's work has connected with those working in professional development and national reform networks. The National Writing Project commissioned Hutchinson to curate an online exhibition of her own and her CASTL colleagues' strategies around teaching reading. She has presented her multimedia website of teaching practice at national conferences on the teaching of English, at the American Educational Research Association annual meeting, and many others. The applicability of her practice to these multiple contexts unveils an opportunity to articulate stronger connections between pre-service teaching, support during the induction years, and ongoing professional development for teachers.

Hutchinson's website grew out of her local colleagues' desire to see into her classroom—to unpack the ways in which she develops her students' competence and the learning community she establishes with her students. This community extends beyond her classroom. In the reflective interview included on the site, viewers can see that Hutchinson sits in her living room at home and reflects on the social justice mission undergirding her practice as her students pass by in the background, using her house for the set of a film they were developing about another book they read in her class.[9] Her community unfolds over time. Hutchinson is in touch with hundreds of former students and speaks proudly of their college scholarships, jobs, and families. By putting her practice online, Hutchinson's work directly informs the preparation of dozens of student teachers every year across the country.

LEARNING FROM AND WITH THE PRACTICE OF PHILLIP LEVIEN

Two hundred miles up the coast from Yvonne Hutchinson, Philip Levien stages two Shakespearean comedies every year during his 50-minute Sheltered English Drama class. His students speak four languages natively, and many of them are mainstreamed into his class with Special Education diagnoses. Levien is a former professional actor[10] and director but has been working to transform students into actors and playwrights at San Marcos High School in Santa Barbara.[11] Because of the fluid nature of the drama course, Levien is free to experiment with pedagogy and curriculum, creating apertures for his students' diversity to enter in and transform the teaching and learning in the classroom. An introduction to *The Comedy of Errors* is presented in English, Spanish, Chinese, and Farsi. Two young men enacting a classic Shakespearean mistaken-identity scene insert a complicated hand-slapping routine upon realizing their resemblance. Overall, this group of students, who might otherwise be categorized as "at risk," challenge themselves to tackle a "gatekeeper" text by becoming the text.

The video footage comprising the majority of classroom data on Phil Levien's website[12] was originally collected by the University of California at Santa Barbara's Center for Education and Social Justice, located in the Gewirtz School of Education. Led by Elizabeth Yeager, the Center created an 8-minute-long video describing Levien's journey with his students to perform *The Comedy of Errors* in fall 2002. However, in order to produce the video, Yeager and her colleagues collected video footage from nearly 20 days of classroom instruction over the course of the semester. Because they had secured permission for the footage to be used online in multiple ways, Yeager and Levien made it available to the Quest Project of the Carnegie Foundation so that it could be incorporated into a website used for the training and development of pre-service secondary English teachers.

On the website, Levien includes a "Director's Note" from his theatrical program in which he describes his impetus to have students learn and perform Shakespeare particularly because Shakespeare's plays are difficult texts.

> Our company of actors is largely comprised of recent arrivals from different countries. One might logically ask: why perform Shakespeare? Why choose such a difficult playwright? My first response is that I wished to select a script that would not privilege the culture of any of the actors over that of the others. Since most of the students are learning English, Shakespeare seemed appropriate. Next, the Bard of Avon is considered to be what educators call a "gatekeeper" author. Students must come to grips with him before passing through the gates of higher education and into the world of rewarding careers. As anyone knows that has read him, he is challenging, to say the least! This production is meant to provide scaffolding for students who will be reading Shakespeare in their English class here at San Marcos, and in college, once they graduate.[13]

The students echo this observation in the UCSB edited video. A young Spanish-speaking student comments that "obviously, you don't know all of the English language. I mean, you have your lines, and if you understand it in your own language, then you know how to react when you say it, and that's where body language comes into it." But beyond the UCSB video, site visitors can become "virtual student teachers" to Levien and his classroom because they can view, rewind, and review multiple days of instruction to see how the production developed—from becoming accustomed to the language of the play, to developing increasing physical comfort in enacting the scenes, and, finally, to creating props, sets, and costumes as the day of the performance approaches.

Levien has also included a great deal of classroom documentation to support and extend the video footage available. Audiences can read through his production notes, investigate the various editions of Shakespeare for school performance that Levien has used, and read students' own one-act plays and scenes inspired by their reading of Shakespeare.

As with Yvonne Hutchinson's website, the development and enactment of competence and community in Levien's classroom occurs in dialect. The stronger the community Levien builds with his students, the stronger their competence and dominion over the difficult text becomes. Just as with Hutchinson's website, placing Levien's work and materials online extends the possibilities for competence and community beyond the walls of his classroom.

When I asked Levien if anything had surprised him about making his teaching practice available online, he shared that two of his students had used the website to demonstrate their own competence to a larger community Levien hadn't anticipated: One student e-mailed the URL of the website to her relatives in China so that they could see her performance and said her relatives were very proud of her developing English skills. Another former student of Levien's, now a truck driver in the rural valleys outside of Santa Barbara, shared the website with his young stepson to show him how hard he'd worked to bring off his performance of Dromeo. Both of these instances underscore how a teacher's work to develop his students' competence attains true luster when the students themselves are fully aware of their hard work and increased competence. His work as their instructor to create a sense of theatrical community is surrounded by invisible filaments connecting each production member to their own networks and their own communities, who can then bear witness to the student's scholarly and artistic work.

LEARNING FROM AND WITH
THE PRACTICE OF JENNIFER MYERS

In Morgan Hill, California, just outside of San Jose, Jennifer Myers is relatively new to teaching. At the time her practice was documented in June 2004, she was only in her fourth year of teaching and had completed her MEd in the prior year. Her school, Barrett Elementary, was brand new the year she was hired to teach 2nd grade, and it has an ethnically and economically diverse student population.[14] The school emphasizes faculty collaboration, and Myers has worked closely over the years with her grade-level cohorts, some novices and some veteran teachers, to develop a rigorous literacy curriculum. The district was chosen to participate in the Every Child a Reader and Writer initiative funded by the Noyce Foundation,[15] which involved intensive professional development and a workshop approach to the teaching of writing. A former professor recommended Jennifer Myers as an exemplary new teacher whose students were strongly responding to the reading and writing workshop method, and the professor thought that others would benefit from seeing how Myers was continuing to develop these practices. This professor had brought groups of students to watch Myers teach and saw that many other teacher groups were passing through the school and Myers's classroom, observing her teaching for their own professional development. Even in the early stages of her career, Myers was becoming a demonstration teacher.

Jennifer Myers's website[16] functions as a "virtual class observation" site— audiences can watch an entire morning of Myers's literacy block: readers' workshop, word study, and writers' workshop. In Myers's classroom, the workshop period begins with a "minilesson" describing a concept or task for the day, a period of independent student work during which Myers meets with students individually or in small groups, and a "shareout" during which the students exchange their work in pairs, small groups, or present it to the entire class. At the beginning of the school year, Myers strongly emphasizes "rituals and routines" for literacy, building a classroom community for academic achievement. For example, the students learn approaches to particular writing genres (such as informational, personal narrative, procedural), how to get help when they're stuck, and how to confer with the teacher and one another to improve their writing. Like many other elementary classrooms, her walls are covered with instructional supports—posters describing what to do when you're done writing, how to select a "Just Right Book," lists of high-frequency words, examples of student writing—and the students continuously consult them as reminders of the community's rituals and routines for learning. The website includes images of all of these supports so that website visitors can see how the students draw upon these scaffolds during their independent work periods.

The website of Myers's work, "Living the Life of a Reader and Writer," wasn't officially linked to the Carnegie Foundation website until June 2006. However, months prior, a development version of the website was up, and several teachers had found her site simply by Googling "video of readers and writers workshop."[17] She started receiving e-mails from all around the world from teachers thanking her for making her work public. Without even intending to, Myers had responded to a void in professional development: images of everyday practice. The response to Myers's work began to illuminate another community: individual teachers worldwide who are hungry to improve their literacy teaching. One teacher e-mailed from Chang Mai, Thailand, saying that she

> stumbled across your website this afternoon while preparing for a teachers' training on reading and writing workshops. I can't believe that you

are such a new teacher! After only a few years you have really got it down! Bravo! . . . I am doing a teacher training when school starts. We have graduated from three teachers to five this coming year, and as the 5th-grade teacher I am hoping to get everyone "on the same page" so that by time the kids get to me they have some basic skills. Until now, it has been every man for himself as far as teaching methods and strategies. Not working, believe me! Sadly, I had a group of 5th graders this year who read at a 2nd-grade level and can't write a sentence, let alone a paragraph or story. They had never really written stories if you can believe it! Anyway, if you wouldn't mind I would like to show your videos to my teachers during our training. They are wonderfully done and so easy to follow.

Another teacher described transforming her literacy practices using Myers's site for guidance:

I am a 3rd-grade teacher in northwest Georgia. This year, I am breaking the norm in my grade level to implement the Workshop model. I have been relentlessly searching for materials and guidance this summer. Your site is wonderful!!!! It has been so helpful to me and so I am sending links to all of my colleagues in hopes that they, too, will be inspired.

Yet another teacher wrote to commend Myers for her bravery in going public with her practice:

I think it is really brave of you to put yourself out there like this so that many of the rest of us can "peek" inside your classroom. One of the worst things about teaching is that they never give you enough time to observe in other classrooms ONCE you become a teacher. You get lots of time when you are a student teacher, but after you've taught for several years, that's when you know what to look for and what you need to reinvigorate your classroom.

Local teachers who have found her site have even e-mailed Myers asking if they can visit her classroom in person. Myers, herself, is part of a vibrant learning community at her school site, and she commented how struck she is by the lack of a sense of community faced by the teachers who contact her about her website:

I can't believe that I'm hearing from people all over the world, really, and they really are yearning for this kind of teaching, this philosophy. In some ways, it makes me a little bit sad that they have to go so far, that they're just not getting that from their administrators or their colleagues.

That they're not able to start book clubs with one another, and they have to go out on their own. I feel very blessed in the sense that I have an awesome principal. Really, I wouldn't be who I am without her really setting the tone of the school. Then also having my second grade team. . . . With our second grade team, and with our entire school, we all team together. We meet once a week and it's not just filling in the blanks in our lesson plan book. We're spending time reflecting together, and planning quality lessons that make sense and meet the needs of all of our students. . . . [I]n addition to all that, we spend time as a staff and we do the book clubs, where . . . one time a week we meet and we read a chapter of a book. Right now we're focusing on math, and we all go, and we give up our lunch, and we talk around what's going on in that chapter and how we can apply it. I think that it's just building community there among the teachers. And that's what was making me sad before, with these teachers contacting me—I'm so excited that they're contacting me, but at the same time, why aren't they getting that same kind of help in their own school, in their own site?

These teachers, and many others who were moved to respond to Myers's work, are part of an invisible community—one that doesn't even realize its own interconnection. These teachers across the country (and the world) who are interested in developing their teaching competence—in this case, literacy workshop practice—have a great deal to gain if they all become "reinvigorated" by gathering around touchstone records of teaching practice like Myers's, Levien's, and Hutchinson's, but even more important, like those yet to be created.

ENVISIONING A NEW KIND OF "COMPETENT COMMUNITY" FOR TEACHING AND LEARNING

By opening up their classrooms to critique and collaboration, these teachers have demonstrated great courage in going public with their teaching practice. They have emphasized the *practices* in their classrooms, the pedagogical and curricular moves through which the learning communities are enacted and that allow students' and teachers' developing competences to be made visible. In doing so, they have laid the foundation for a new kind of professional community for teaching—one that does not depend on geographical proximity or the cultivation of personal relationships, but which emerges from a growing number of educators who are hungry for collaborative colleagues, classrooms with open doors, and images of possible practices that they might adapt to their own contexts. Once that community begins to unveil itself, a new conception of what it means to learn from and in practice will surely follow.

NOTES

1. See http://carnegiefoundation.org/programs/index.asp?key=32 for more about the CASTL program.

2. King-Drew enrolls 1,600 students in grades 9–12. Its student population is 66% African American and 33% Latino.

3. See http://gallery.carnegiefoundation.org/collections/quest/collections/sites/ divans-hutchinson_yvonne/anticipationguide.html

4. See http://gallery.carnegiefoundation.org/collections/quest/collections/sites/ divans-hutchinson_yvonne/yvonne2dv8.mov for Hutchinson's students' discussion of this plot point.

5. See http://gallery.carnegiefoundation.org/collections/quest/collections/sites/ divans-hutchinson_yvonne/ydhreflection.mov

6. See http://quest.carnegiefoundation.org/~pgrossman/ for more about Grossman's use of Hutchinson's website.

7. See http://quest.carnegiefoundation.org/~kschultz/ for more about Schultz's use of Hutchinson's website.

8. See http://quest.carnegiefoundation.org/~arichert/ for more about Richert's use of Hutchinson's website.

9. See http://gallery.carnegiefoundation.org/collections/quest/collections/sites/ divans-hutchinson_yvonne/ydhreflection.mov

10. See http://www.imdb.com/name/nm0505524/

11. San Marcos High enrolls 2,077 students in grades 9–12. Its student population is 51% White, 41% Hispanic, and 4% Asian and Filipino.

12. See http://gallery.carnegiefoundation.org/collections/quest/collections/ sites/levien_phil/

13. See http://gallery.carnegiefoundation.org/collections/quest/collections/ sites/levien_phil/learningandperforming.htm

14. Barrett enrolls 543 students in grades K–6. Its student population is 46% Hispanic, 38% White, 5% Asian, and 2% African American.

15. See http://noycefdn.org/literacy/index.html

16. See http://gallery.carnegiefoundation.org/collections/quest/collections/ sites/myers_jennifer/

17. See http://www.google.com/search?hl=en&rlz=1B3GGGL_enUS217US218&q =readers+writers+workshop+video&btnG=Search

6

The New Teacher Center Forum: Developing a Community of Practice

Ellen Moir
Susan Hanson

The New Teacher Center (NTC) at the University of California, Santa Cruz, began in 1998 as an outgrowth of the Santa Cruz New Teacher Project (SCNTP). Begun by a small group of teacher educators, SCNTP staff wanted to transform the way new teachers enter the profession through mentor-based induction. Our work was conceived in response to mentoring programs in which experienced educators were simply paired with new teachers on an informal basis using a "buddy system" model. Mentors were neither trained for their new role nor given time to carry out its demands. Similar to new teachers, they had to sink or swim, armed with only intuition and good intentions to keep themselves afloat.

The NTC's theory of teacher development emphasizes ongoing skill and knowledge growth focused on building student success in communities of practice. New teachers need an intensive induction program focused on instruction and the guidance of successful, experienced teachers trained to accelerate the advancement of their classroom practice. Experienced teachers can become effective mentors and school leaders, but the kind of professional development offered to them matters immensely. Quality mentoring requires a broad knowledge base that includes the ability to build adult relationships, both with individuals and among groups; a commitment to collaboration; and the skills to articulate teaching strategies, analyze evidence, and support teacher growth and development. Both mentors and new teachers need time off from other duties to work to improve their practice.

OVERVIEW OF THE NTC MODEL

The crux of the NTC's strategy is strong mentoring and coaching within a culture that emphasizes the continuous learning of all professionals in the system. Mentoring is ultimately a teaching role—teachers teaching teachers to teach, and like classroom teaching, it is complex work. We encourage the districts with whom we work to release exemplary experienced teachers full time from the classroom to mentor approximately 13 to 15 novice teachers and participate in a learning community of mentors for at least 2 years. The teachers selected to be mentors improve their knowledge and skills simultaneously with sustained investment in their training that exposes them to professional norms and innovative classroom practices.

The key elements of the NTC's model are (1) one-to-one mentoring, (2) formative assessment, (3) mentor professional development, and (4) a community of practice. Our multilayered approach to professional learning yields an expanded knowledge base for the mentors, experience participating in a professional learning community, and an inquiry orientation that supports collaborative learning communities in schools.

Experienced teachers mentoring new teachers full time is a relatively new teacher leadership role in schools. Gaining the support of districts to release teachers full time has allowed us to experiment with a structure that brings these teachers together to better understand beginning teacher needs, mentor development, and how to support the teaching profession. Writing this chapter has pushed us to ask important questions about our work supporting mentors and deconstruct our success supporting their development. We want to be more explicit about our work so others can successfully build upon it. For this chapter, we have asked ourselves, what are the Forum's essential features that support the mentor's work? What is the process by which the NTC teacher learning communities develop and thrive? There is so much talk about learning communities, but learning communities that build safe communities of practice and competence are not very well understood.

FORMATIVE ASSESSMENT: A CONTINUOUS IMPROVEMENT CYCLE FOR MENTORS AND NEW TEACHERS

Mentors have as a primary goal to construct authentic inquiry-oriented learning with their beginning teachers. The NTC Formative Assessment System (FAS) provides a set of protocols and tools for the new teacher and mentor to collect objective, useful evidence to examine and analyze together. The NTC model emphasizes not telling beginning teachers where to improve, but inquiring with them about their practice and tailoring support to the assessed instructional needs of the beginning teacher. By working together to improve classroom pedagogical practices, beginning teachers and mentors see how working together improves competence.

The quality of the mentor–teacher relationship is at the core of mentor work. Mentoring requires building trust with new teachers, looking for entry points, and helping teachers to reflect upon their pedagogical practices to build their competence. The Formative Assessment tools provide a framework for guided conversations between mentors and novices that help teachers reflect on their own practice. As mentors work with their new teachers in small groups using a shared set of instructional principles and strategies, they begin to create school cultures in which sharing to improve one's practice becomes the norm. The Formative Assessment structure encourages schools to establish norms of inquiry and reflection that support teachers to collaboratively work together to improve classroom instruction.

THE NEW TEACHER CENTER'S
APPROACH TO PROFESSIONAL LEARNING

Few teachers, no matter how exemplary their classroom practice, are prepared to assume the role of mentor teacher in an ambitious induction program without participating in considerable professional learning. From the inception of our program, we recognized the need to support our mentors who were assuming a brand-new role. Designing a comprehensive induction program requires designing a parallel program to train and support the mentors. We asked ourselves the following kinds of questions with regards to the mentors: What are the essential understandings and skills that would best support mentors in their work? How can we support the leadership and passion of experienced teachers in their role as mentors? How can we create the context for ongoing learning? These questions helped shape the curriculum and our strategies for mentor development. The initial school districts with whom we worked released experienced schoolteachers to join our consortium. We started with only four mentors working in Santa Cruz County schools. Ellen met with the mentors every week to study the beginning teachers' progress and understand the mentors' needs. We studied their initial work together. Because these mentors were on loan to the program, they had a need to create a community, just as they had when they were teachers in the schools. None of us had supported new teachers when we began. Ellen Moir, as Director of Teacher Education at UC Santa Cruz, had supported pre-service teachers and the mentors had been classroom teachers. The mentors were accomplished teachers, but they didn't really know what it was about their practice that made them good teachers. Together we learned that mentors have a need to study the metacognitive process of teaching to make explicit what they did correctly, as well as identify what knowledge and skills new teachers need. This is how we came to develop our community of practice. It has been essential to our work since we began, but with just five of us beginning to understand what it means to implement a high-quality induction program, it was less structured.

Through our community of practice, NTC has developed a curriculum of professional development for mentors that includes a variety of tools to help new teachers to examine their own classroom practice, analyze student work, engage in active listening and coaching, analyze a teacher's performance based on professional teaching standards, and assess mentor growth and development. Mentors also read and discuss issues such as differentiated instruction, equity, standards-based education, and working with special needs populations. The NTC's tools and topics continue to be expanded and refined as we grow our program.

THE MENTOR FORUM

Our core structure for developing a professional community of practice among mentors is the Mentor Forum, a weekly 3-hour professional learning opportunity for mentors. It is rooted in the fundamental principles of effective professional development, reinforces our induction goals, and teaches the structures and processes that are at the core of the NTC model. The Mentor Forum provides a mechanism by which mentors gain cognitive knowledge and bring forth issues of practice into the larger community of mentors. Here is what a few mentors say regarding knowledge they gained in the Forum:

> It [the Forum] has really developed my mental cognitive process. It's about becoming more conscious of teaching practices—I think that's a good way to generalize it—in every area of teaching, all the different principles. I was doing a lot of things instinctually, but this has really forced me to evaluate why I made the choices in the classrooms that I did.

> I think the training that I went through to become a mentor is training that every teacher should receive. What a classroom should look like, what reflection should look like, what lesson planning should look like . . . I've learned so much in my training about how to become a better teacher because these are things we want to see in our teachers. I feel like *if I went back into the classroom now, I'd be a much better teacher than I ever was.*

> It seems like everything is objective based and there's a purpose and a clear goal or objective. . . . It makes me feel that my time is being spent in a worthwhile manner.

Each Mentor Forum is established thoughtfully with an agenda intended to increase mentor competence and norms that contribute to developing a rich learning community. The weekly agenda includes Connecting, Problem Pose/Problem Solve, a New Learning, Reflection, and Feedback for Future Forums.

The Connecting activity is a way to bring in the voices and experience of the mentors. It draws on the mentor's prior knowledge and connects to the content of the Forum.

The Problem Pose/Problem Solve activity brings groups of mentors together to share a current problem or dilemma, receive feedback, and then switch roles. Such on-the-ground exchanges regarding immediate issues are meaningful for the mentors and set a tone and a way of thinking that helps them feel that they are part of a community of colleagues to whom they can turn to for support. This structure engages mentors in authentic discussion, highlights the knowledge of mentors, and ultimately builds their competence and trust in one another, as reflected in the comments below:

> Most every Wednesday we meet and there is always something that we talk about. What have your challenges been this week? What have your successes been and how did you handle that?

> They [the mentors] are just so creative; the ideas we come up with. And, also they are problem solvers; I respect that. . . . It's confidential, anything we talk about. So if we're having a problem in our school with an ILT [new teacher], we could talk. We would get in little small groups and have our little time to talk about them. Mentors give their ideas and strategies.

As you might imagine, a large variety of challenges and problems are shared in these sessions. Here are some examples of those challenges:

- Supporting teachers who are feeling overwhelmed and discouraged after a few months of teaching, especially if they are working in a "sanctioned" school. How can mentors support the teacher to move forward without only sharing one's personal opinion?
- Supporting teachers in establishing a contributing role on their grade-level or department team. Even more challenging: helping them establish a role on a solid team where they feel inadequate or helping to improve a dysfunctional team.
- Supporting a "nonelect" teacher whose contract will probably not be renewed. Mentors often learn about this status before the teacher does and they must not only keep it confidential, but also find ways to help the teacher maintain morale and teach to the best of his or her ability.
- Helping teachers shift perspective of their role and deepen their definition of themselves as professional educators. Mentors are responsible

for helping teachers see their work not just as classroom teachers, but also as part of a profession with a larger purpose.

- Helping new teachers develop a repertoire of skills in new teachers who are not making much progress. Mentors want to know how to support their development.

After mentors share in pairs, there is a group sharing so everyone can benefit. The Problem Pose/Problem Solve activity also provides a template for a process of sharing and reflecting that teachers can take to their schools and use with whomever they work.

The New Learning section of the Forum provides mentors the opportunity to focus on the pedagogy of mentoring and content theme that supports professional learning. NTC's curriculum is grounded in the everyday practice and needs of new teachers and is responsive to local context and program needs. By meeting regularly with the mentors, program directors and NTC lead mentors hear about common challenges that teachers face (such as differentiating instruction for English language learners, integrating literacy skills into content areas, and using assessment to inform pedagogy). The Formative Assessment System used by the mentor and new teacher to collect evidence of practice and examine it together becomes a source of information for NTC to understand the needs of new teachers and develop our curriculum. The cycle of inquiry that mentors use with teachers results in a parallel cycle of inquiry among mentors when they share data they collected at the schools with each other; this, in turn, helps us identify topics we want to include in the Forums.

The Formative Assessment System tools used in the Mentor Forum provide a framework for guided conversations between mentors and novices that helps teachers reflect on their own practice. In California there are 20 Induction Program Standards that mentors must comprehend well and use adeptly in conversations with new teachers to facilitate authentic learning. One of our program challenges is to help mentors use the tools and the standards in a manner that engages each new teacher while meeting his or her individual needs. When not implemented well, the standards become merely a list to check off as the school year progresses. The more the mentors know, the deeper they can engage in analyzing the beginning teachers' and other mentors' work. Building more competence within the community of mentors leads to a more effective learning community.

BUILDING A COMMUNITY OF PRACTICE

In addition to increasing the knowledge base and skills of mentors, the weekly Forums provide regular opportunities for collaborative learning and inquiry. The Forums support mentors to become agents of their own professional growth through working with a community of other professional educators.

> On Fridays those 3-hour staff development meetings were unbelievable because they don't usually happen at schools. . . . The professional development staff meetings were really a model for me, as far as trying to bring that feeling back into the schools. . . . The feeling of being honored as a professional, the feeling of being able to study something, discuss it with your peers, and maybe implement some tiny change in your practice from being kind of nurtured in that environment.

> I'm in a community of people that are encouraged to think, to share their thinking, to analyze, to contribute, to create, to reflect, to discuss. We are given that space, which I guess you can call time. It's like having a mentor. Our mentor forums are where we meet for 3 hours to come together. It's broken up with some kind of professional development, some kind of reflection, some kind of disseminating information . . . but we're not pushed. . . . There's a human quality to this that doesn't exist in the teaching profession.

The Mentor Forum provides a place for accomplished teachers who have different areas of expertise across subject areas and schools to work together to build their competence within a community of practice. The Mentor Forum gives these teachers a chance to come across subject areas and boundaries to focus on new teacher development and their own learning. Mentors are encouraged to share their curriculum, subject matter, and pedagogical expertise in response to expressed needs of the mentor community.

> The brilliance of this learning community is that it's a generalist-perspective mentoring as opposed to subject-specific. If it was subject specific, [as a music teacher] I would never need to talk to the English teacher. . . . The NTC structure necessitates collaboration. . . . I'm a music guy; I'm ill equipped to [mentor] a core subject new teacher unless I get some information on that, and I can think of no better place to do that than to go talk to somebody with 20 years of experience. . . . I want to go talk to the experts and we have all the experts in the room. . . . It's a room of competent people, all cheering for the same goals and all supportive of one another.

> The respect [I have for my colleagues] leads to a willingness to listen, to accept what someone else may have to offer. . . . [W]hat they have to offer doesn't necessarily mean that you are lacking in any way. I feel that you can't be good at everything. We have a conglomerate here, so you take a little bit from wherever you can.

It's not anything I've ever really been a part of—such a large group of people who want to contribute to one another's development.

Just as mentoring is about experienced teachers supporting new teachers, the Mentor Forum offers mentors a chance to learn together about mentoring. Accomplished teachers experience many new responsibilities and challenges as new mentors, and during the Forum they share their learning in pairs and triads across grade levels and subject matters. There is intersubjectivity that develops because they are all mentoring novice teachers and trying to accelerate the novices' development. Mentors view their work as a collective responsibility to support novice teachers across the district.

The Forum develops a culture of respect that leads to learning, and participants gain a deep understanding of what a community of practice looks and feels like. Mentors informally organize and work together outside of the Forum to be more effective, and this reinforces their sense of community.

We really had to become tight in order to build the best support for our mentees and their needs. . . . For example, I have teachers that are from kindergarten on to fifth [grade]. I have a P.E. teacher; I have an art teacher. So, I've had to team up in some cases with the music [mentor] teacher and the P.E. [mentor] teacher to support these teachers.

We've gotten together and done some problem solving and observations. I went over to another mentor's school [and] observed her, and then we sat down and talked about some of the things that I might do [in her position]. I've had mentors come and shadow me all day to see how I do my mentoring.

Working with other mentors has probably been one of the most positive things about this program. As professionals building a common language and understanding about teaching and learning, mentors find [in] each other great sources of expertise and support.

Even though we see each other less frequently, I have more contact and more meaningful interaction professionally with these 31 other people than I did on campus as a teacher. We are in constant e-mail contact with one another. We see one another. . . . We ask, "Can you help me out?" They are the most willing people to help another person I've ever met in this profession. . . . They are so open to helping one another learn, and [they have] that "I might not have answers, but we'll work together" kind of attitude. . . . I look forward to it every week.

What makes me feel like I'm part of a community? . . . Number one: sharing, sharing, and sharing. And, it seems like everything is objective based and there's a purpose and a clear goal or objective.

The mentors, as accomplished teachers themselves, take pride in helping beginning teachers to improve their practices. Their mutual focus on doing the same work and their recognition that they each have skills and knowledge that can support one another's learning help them to develop deep, instructional relationships with colleagues and build habits of inquiry.

FORUM MEETINGS SUPPORT
MENTOR LEADERSHIP DEVELOPMENT

Each Forum meeting has a content theme, and mentors are asked to plan and facilitate portions of each meeting. Mentors are encouraged to take leadership roles from the initial connecting activity to teaching new concepts and effective strategies. They receive guidance from lead mentors and the project director. Teachers, upon assuming the mentor role, often have not had much experience presenting workshops or facilitating teacher learning communities. Leading parts of the weekly Forum gives mentors leadership experience that will serve them well at their school sites and in their careers. Mentors also lead one another in collaborative working groups on tasks that have important implications for teacher induction in their district.

> Everybody is on a committee. We have five committees where we're looking at next steps for next year and the continuation of this program. . . . There are six or seven of us and it's amazing what we've accomplished.

As teachers lead teachers in doing tasks they have never done, all participants gain a better sense of what authentic, collaborative learning looks like.

> This experience has forced me to do things that I've never done before, and it's provided the support to do that. . . . [Instead of just saying] "Do it," I'm getting the training and I have the support of my colleagues.

THE PROGRAM LEADER'S ROLE
IN MENTOR DEVELOPMENT

When mentors join our community they have rarely experienced a true professional community. We continue to reflect upon why this is. Experienced teachers have all had professional development "done to them." Traditionally, they have come out of a system that is predominantly top-down where someone makes the decision about what they need to learn. Their mentoring experience in the Forum demonstrates that there is another way. While teachers appreciate the opportunity to meet with their colleagues, successful learning communities do not simply develop as a result of establishing a weekly meeting. Mentors can easily become cynical of weekly meetings that take time away from their primary charge to support novice teachers at school sites. NTC's vision of a successful weekly Forum is quite different than the traditional school staff meeting. Mentor Forums are not staff meetings. We continually reflect and ask ourselves and the mentors "What do mentors need to know?" We continue to co-construct the Forums.

It takes excellent leadership skills, an ability to be a learner and a teacher, and a vision of the potential power of such a community to establish a successful mentor learning community. Mentors, selected districtwide, recognize the talent in the room. They are excited about their new role, but may be skeptical from past experience. The program leader must earn the respect of the experienced teachers to make the most of the collective skills and potential of the group to serve their district. Here is how a few mentors described the skills of a successful leader who makes them feel valued:

> It's a very positive environment where I feel valued. I feel like everybody feels valued and that everyone's input is valued. I guess he [the program director] does it by modeling. He takes whatever comes his way, whether he agrees or disagrees, [and] puts it on the table. I'm not always sure we can tell whether he agrees or disagrees. I guess that's kind of a neat thing. He puts the ideas on the table and then lets the group work through it.

> The way he [the program director] has incorporated us into the development of things that are coming and the way we've been asked to contribute our ideas at the district level, I think that has made people feel very professional and that their knowledge is highly regarded. . . . [A]s a result, [he] has inspired a lot of people to want to learn together . . . and contribute together.

The program leader of the NTC learning community must be able to facilitate learning among its participants. When the leadership is didactic, the mentors are more likely to consider the weekly meetings not worth their time. Mentors must have an opportunity to bring their problems and dilemmas from the field to the Mentor Forum and hear the suggestions of their colleagues. This time spent together solving immediate problems and learning from one another builds trust and an authentic learning environment. A successful mentor community becomes a sanctuary where mentors find a positive learning experience well worth their time. Having this satisfying experience becomes a model for the types of communities in which they want to work. A mentor explained:

> When I facilitate my meetings [with mentees], I want to do what he [the program director] does here [in the Mentor Forum]. . . . I'd love to have a

list of the things he does that make our atmosphere wonderful. If I could take that and model that for my teachers, then they could take it and model it in their classrooms or in their communities. . . . I can't put my finger on it, but part of it is that valuing and remaining objective. . . . It's a very professional community.

The NTC model envisions the mentor community eventually running it-self. Mentors have opportunities to take on new roles and responsibilities as the program matures and grows. The mentors, if properly selected, are among the most talented and skilled teachers in their district, most with capabilities to lead. It is the program director's responsibility to build norms and process-es that enable everyone to emerge as leaders and acquire experience. When leadership opportunities emerge, the program director will usually find him-self or herself in the precarious position of having to choose among many talented people for a limited number of coveted assignments. This can be a challenging, uncomfortable task for the program director. The more the men-tor community can assume responsibility and leadership for its own work and expansion, the more opportunities it will have to distribute a variety of responsibilities among its members.

The learning community created by the Mentor Forum is a prototype for the kind of culture that we want mentors to help create in the schools. Strong leadership, powerful tools, and a process that values the wisdom of the men-tors are essential to successfully implementing our model.

CONCLUSION

Writing this chapter has pushed us to reflect on how we built this community and how our mentors work to build competence and community. The experi-ence has shown us that there is a need to develop explicit language about how to develop teacher learning communities that can sustain themselves. One of the major things we have learned is how important the leader is in model-ing inquiry—by asking important questions, by engaging teachers to build on their knowledge and co-construct the work, and by using teachers to build a new body of knowledge. If we want a group that inquires, the leader has to inquire. If we believe that formative assessment data and the continuous im-provement process are important for new teacher and mentor development, then we have to figure out how to build in the time and skills to analyze the work. The Forum is a place where we attempt to walk our talk. It is a place where we try to live through example the importance of teacher expertise in pushing the teaching profession forward.

Even after 19 years of facilitating strong induction programs, we are still gaining insights about professional learning and community building in schools. A healthy induction system is constantly gathering feedback and using the creativity and experiences of its participants to reshape itself from year to year. Looking at the outcomes of our work in several school districts and moving back to our theory of action helps us be more intentional and explicit about what we want to accomplish. We see how building communities of practice and building competence in mentors can have a powerful impact on entire communities, from classrooms to schools. Through strong mentoring and coaching, educators can work more purposefully together on many levels to create and support communities of adult learners in schools.

7

Increasing Elementary Teachers' Fundamental Math Content Knowledge and Developing a Collaborative Faculty

Matt Ellinger

The following is a story of a group of teachers at a single school who reached new heights as a collaborative faculty. The vehicle for this transformation was a shared commitment to broadening their own (not just their students') knowledge of mathematics. Even with the fears, the embarrassment, and the stigma of being someone who "just never got it," these teachers grew professionally in important ways. Notice in the coming pages the shifts in their patterns of professional isolation, collegial communication, internal motivation, and even their own identities as learners of mathematics.

In July 2003, Liping Ma invited me to help navigate her through the professional lives of about 25 teachers at a California public school not far from San Jose. Her plan was to facilitate a process similar to Lesson Study among the teachers and to explore the mathematics they were teaching. I accepted Dr. Ma's offer and spent the next 3 years working with her and with a wonderful group of devoted professionals at a local elementary school. The teachers ranged in age and experience. They differed in teaching philosophies and approaches. They excelled in some aspects of their jobs and struggled in others. In short, they were normal. And "normal" for most elementary teachers also means that they had not yet had the opportunity or the desire to study mathematics in depth. In fact, many of the teachers reported to me that distaste for mathematics was a factor in their selecting the elementary school level, implying that the knowledge necessary to teach young children mathematics is not consequential.

FUNDAMENTAL, NOT BASIC, MATHEMATICS

But it *is* consequential. Liping Ma (1999) distinguishes the understandings of teachers about mathematics through discussion of the *basic* and the *fundamental* points of view. When K–5 school mathematics is viewed as *basic* mathematics, the mathematics is described as a collection of procedures. When it is viewed as *fundamental*, the mathematics is described as *elementary* (the beginning of the discipline), *primary* (containing the rudiments of advanced mathematics) and *foundational* (supporting future learning). Supporting the *fundamental* point of view, Ma argues that elementary teachers require a "profound understanding of fundamental mathematics" that has breadth, depth, and thoroughness (p. 116).

Deborah Ball (2003) goes further. For more than 20 years she and her team have been working to illuminate with precision what teachers must know to teach math well. She has also been working on how to teach it to teachers and how to measure whether teachers have learned it. But what is the *it*? Ball (2003) calls it Mathematical Knowledge for Teaching (MKT). In her comments made at the U.S. Department of Education's Summit on Mathematics,[1] Dr. Ball concluded that "teachers need to know the same things that we would want any educated member of our society to know, but much more." She goes on to remind us, "The mathematical problems and challenges of teaching are not the same as those faced by engineers, nurses, physicists, or astronauts." And this leads to her central point: "The mathematical knowledge needed for teaching must be usable for those mathematical problems."

In describing Ball's decrying of the nonthinking-based approaches to teaching, such as the too common "just bring down the zero" explanation, Debra Viadero shares in her 2004 *Education Week* article: "This is no mere academic hairsplitting. . . . Her research shows that students whose teachers score high on the measures developed by Ms. Ball and her research partners learn more math over the school year than do students of low-scoring teachers" (p. 8).

Both Ma and Ball attribute Lee Shulman with inspiring their study of elementary mathematics teaching. Shulman's (1987) theory of Pedagogical Content Knowledge (PCK) refers to the idea that teachers need to know content in a way that differs from other experts in order to teach it well. So, it was with a mission to provide teachers with the underlying content necessary for PCK or MKT that Liping Ma and I entered into the workings of a modest, at times struggling, California elementary school.

MATHEMATICS CONTENT
WITHIN PROFESSIONAL DEVELOPMENT

There were parallel purposes of Liping Ma devoting her time to Slater Elementary School. In addition to teacher learning goals, she had important research questions regarding the day-to-day work of teachers. But instead of taking an observer stance, she elected to become a member of the school's professional community and hired me to come along for the ride. She hoped that the teachers' scheduled weekly grade-level collaborative meetings could become a time when teachers would engage in the process of group planning, debriefing from frequent peer observation, reviewing the work of students, and learning advanced fundamental mathematical concepts related to their grade level.

Ma also was eager to collect data for analysis of how math content is introduced in a "real" school and how she could more directly connect the elements of Profound Understanding of Fundamental Mathematics (PUFM) to authentic teaching tasks. She also was concerned with how teachers would respond to ongoing mathematics instruction and how to deliver instruction to them in ways that did not seem daunting, burdensome, or irrelevant. And finally, Ma was eager to utilize technology in novel ways. She developed a system of virtual observation with the use of video, blogs, and animated examples of mathematics concepts and expressions.

Joining Ma for this work was especially helpful to my professional learning as a school administrator. I was eager to explore whether this school could shift its concept of collaboration from that of simply solving logistical problems as a group to the sharing of knowledge in a way similar to other professional practitioners who work in complex clinical situations. Specifically, teachers at this school perceived collaboration as a vehicle to "lighten the load" of a very difficult job by allowing work to be more efficiently shared. The hope we had is that this entirely valid existing notion of how to collaborate would evolve to become more scientific—meaning that data were gathered, new knowledge pursued, and a spirit of investigation and experimentation encouraged. The disclosure of dilemmas encountered in the classroom would be fuel for discourse and welcomed as a professional challenge to be explored as a team. I also entered into the project wondering about how teachers might benefit from reflecting together about the teaching and learning of mathematics that happens in their classrooms and among themselves as adult learners.

GETTING STARTED

The Mountain View–Whisman School District had worked with their teachers in previous years to establish a designated meeting time for weekly grade-level collaboration. The principal of Slater School, Dr. Nicki Smith, promoted the idea of devoting this collaboration period to working with Dr. Ma and myself. Dr. Smith first encouraged the kindergarten and 1st-grade teachers to participate. This decision was based in part on the idea that the younger students' progress could be measured at the same site over time, but she also chose the teachers she felt would participate most enthusiastically and, in a sense, "sell" the collaborative studying of math to teachers of the older grades. Teachers at the school were already familiar with Lesson Study as a form of professional development. Describing the opportunity as something similar, jokingly termed "Lesson Study Light," helped quell the anxiety regarding mathematics many elementary teachers experience. During our time with the teachers, the focus was divided equally between (1) mathematics content instruction for teachers and (2) teaching and learning mathematics with children. As facilitators of the professional development, we found it critical to tread carefully in both areas. Humility and sensitivity to the work of the teachers was of the utmost importance.

During the content focus of the work, Ma and I explained her theory that the mathematical understanding necessary to teach elementary school math effectively is highly specialized knowledge that very few can truly explore as effectively as they can as elementary teachers. Their ability to reconcile the errors made in written work to remediate appropriately, their fluid examples to bridge concepts, and their well-honed communication skills to make complex ideas manageable are all advantageous professional skills that develop over time. However, Ma contended that experience is *not* the only requisite for gaining this elementary math teacher skill set. There is also unique mathematical material that, once explored and understood, supports the work of being an elementary teacher who introduces young students to a number of mathematical concepts. Not only that, but this material is not readily understood by anyone *except* elementary teachers due to their perspective and experience.

During the time we focused on the practice of the teachers, Ma and I had to establish a climate that, like Lesson Study, invited direct communication among teachers about the strengths and weaknesses apparent in the work of their teaching. There are excellent resources for school professionals to study ways to promote a culture of collaboration among faculty, but Ma and I were outsiders and wanted to become insiders in the school community quickly. After an initial phase of visits and observations to learn about the school, we began teaching children math at every opportunity that the teachers felt was appropriate. Ma would videotape my teaching and I would do the same for her. Next, we would show clips of our teaching at the weekly meetings and speak in detail of how ineffective particular choices were and asked the teachers to come up with suggestions for improvement. We did this in spite of the teachers' inclination to be highly complimentary. In fact, we encouraged a skeptical, yet respectful, stance. In an early videotape of me teaching, Ma found that I was actually confounding a teaching problem by offering inconsistent examples of how a child could conceive of an addition word problem. In front of the teachers, Ma went on to explain to me that with 5- and 6-year-olds the action of joining and the action of increasing are not interchangeable. They need to be handled as discrete ideas and must be thoughtfully blended into a larger concept of addition. I actually did not know this, and it was a great example of how my 20 years in the classroom with older kids did not prepare me for this subtle, yet crucial, mathematical distinction with the little ones. This example of Ma and me engaged in respectful, yet quite direct, feedback regarding teaching and math was crucial in allaying the teachers' fears of judgment when they opened up about their own teaching later. It was very important to resist the urge to "fix" problems the teachers were having in the classroom prior to the development of a focused and collaborative facilitated meeting time.

FACILITATED MEETINGS

Teachers at Slater School devoted alternating weeks' grade-level collaboration sessions to what they termed the Math Lesson Study Project. Strictly speaking, the project only slightly resembled Lesson Study in the manner most often seen in the United States. Ma and I presented a mathematics topic to the teachers and moved to discussing their understanding of the mathematics gradually. We attempted to enter each mathematical area from an unfamiliar angle that helped the teachers feel as if they were on similar footing regardless of the depth of their content knowledge. For example, we traced how children develop the ability to compare quantities and how this ability can be supported through a thoughtful sequence of instruction. This particular set of mathematical concepts seems quite simple when considered superficially, yet it is remarkably complex and fundamental. As a former 3rd-grade teacher, I marveled at the groundwork necessary for the kind of abstraction that I had expected from my students. I also bemoaned the fact that I was guilty of teaching the questionable strategy that "'compare' means 'subtraction'" when solving word problems, for again "finding the difference" and "comparing" are *related* ideas, not *interchangeable*. Well, now I know. The kindergarten and 1st-grade teachers also studied counting, numbers, equations, meanings of subtraction and addition, place value, and story problems. Second through 5th-grade teachers studied similar topics, but with some adjustments to include multiplication and division, formulas, rational numbers, and a few other topics typically introduced a bit later. Often, however, grade-level groups would mix to discuss ways to prepare the younger students in the most helpful way for future instruction. The teachers also found a problem-solving approach similar to that of Hungarian mathematician George Polya (1988) to be an especially helpful method to teach at all grade levels when parsing word problems. Briefly, the approach was (1) Understand the question; (2) Record the data; (3) Develop a plan; (4) Formulate an answer; and (5) Check the answer.

PEER OBSERVATION AND COLLABORATION

Similar to Lesson Study, participating teachers engaged in a cycle of planning, observing, and debriefing as they addressed a particular area of mathematics they felt was particularly confusing or problematic to teach. One example was the 1st-grade teachers working with the students in generating all the additions that equate a particular number, such as 12. This was a rich area to explore because the concept can be approached in a variety of ways and supported by diagrams and manipulatives. The students also generated work that could be assessed and compared. Good research questions arose from the work about whether to start with a group of 12 objects and separate them systematically or to start with the commonly memorized double addition (6 + 6) and adjust up and down, or to use trial and error, number lines, and many more ideas. The teachers tested approaches with each other and argued the validity and compatibility of those they would use. They also questioned how they could relate this all to subtraction. They were off and running on this topic, as they would be later with a number of other topics throughout the project.

After initial discussion, teachers usually grouped into teams of three. Together they would plan a lesson. Shortly thereafter, one teacher would volunteer to teach the lesson to her students and her colleagues would make arrangements to observe the lesson. Immediately following the lesson, teachers would gather again. This time the teachers would discuss how the lesson did or did not succeed in achieving the desired student work. Together, they examined the work that they collected, pointed out significant moments in the teaching, and began the process of altering the lesson to be taught a second and a third time with modifications they determined were likely to support even greater student learning. When possible, these lessons were videotaped to assist the teachers in more thorough analyses and to allow teachers to share clips with one another. The video also served Liping Ma's research, as well, and provided compelling examples in later presentations to the teachers during the facilitated meetings.

ONLINE JOURNALING

The use of a participant blog also served the project well. The teachers made hundreds of entries that included questions, comments, compliments, and concerns. They also used the blog to pose questions about student errors and to share lesson plans. Photographs of charts, graphs, bulletin boards, and manipulatives were also quite popular. The following are three entries among many that demonstrate a highly professional stance regarding continuous learning as a classroom teacher:

> *Teacher A:* For some reason I became absurdly nervous yesterday, even though I am used to Matt taping and all. It was very silly. Nevertheless, I still think this is such a great thing to be able to do, to have the opportunity to see each other teach. When I watched Alice's lesson, I learned so much about being sure the children understand the real heart of the les-

son. I had forgotten to focus on the comparison aspect of the problems, so seeing her do that really made me more aware of that. I also liked the way she had made the planning process of the math problem like making a cake so that the children could understand more clearly just exactly what they were up to. We are making math soufflés!

This morning I was reflecting on this whole year and it struck me that it is a very good thing for the students to see that their teachers are actively still engaged in learning more, and . . . that we are interested in their thinking and [in] helping them to learn to articulate their thinking. This is so important. It gives the school day a more vital feel to it. We are not just spewing out a script we learned from a teacher's manual but . . . are closely observing one another and our children to be sure that we are on the right track. For me, it makes the experience more alive and meaningful, even if I do get ridiculously nervous. I'm still glad that the children are seeing us model this interest in learning and . . . becoming better at what we do. I think they do sense that we value them and their educational progress.

Teacher B: That was a great session yesterday! I really feel like my brain got a workout. Whew! Today, when I composed the word problems for the day, I consciously thought [about] which kind they were. Today, I did . . . combining and an increasing. Now, when I am thinking of them, I am going to really reflect on what I am doing and what I want the children to learn. This is so exciting for me. Liping, I just want to thank you for this wonderful opportunity to learn how to be a better teacher. You truly are a master teacher! Thank you very much.

Teacher C: I found Liping's talk about Zone of Proximal Development [Vygotsky, 1978] to be very interesting, and I was struck with the significance of ZPD for all learning, whether it [is] literacy acquisition, second language acquisition, or mathematical understanding. This is one reason I have some trouble if I am following a rigid lesson plan. I feel that I am constantly trying to monitor and interpret the children's understanding so that I will know I am in their ZPD. That is what I meant by trying to find the "balance." Often they will give me clues right in the midst of what we are doing that it is either too high or too low. I then proceed from there, but I realize that what I do can be kind of sloppy in technique. That worries me a lot.

One thing that Liping said made me feel a little uncomfortable. It was regarding Sue's lesson. . . . Liping felt that it had perhaps become too redundant during the part of writing the equations and [suggested that] the ante could have been raised. I would like for us to discuss this. Did Sue feel that way about that part of the lesson or were the children still engaged with enthusiasm? I have often found that children of this age enjoy practicing what they have just mastered. I would like to hear Sue's response to this question. I guess I just don't want to push them too fast. Or maybe I don't push hard enough.

I also enjoyed the discussion about whether we say *number sentence*, *equation*, or *mathematical expression*. It is so fascinating to have a mathematician of Liping's caliber give us her insights on issues like this. I think I [understand] why she preferred *expression*, but I think that term might be a little ambiguous for our young children. It occurred to me that, since we teach them that a sentence "tells," perhaps *number sentence* would work for them at this stage of their development. The number sentence "tells" us whether the two sides of the equal sign are equal.

I selected these entries because they address three important distinct issues. Teacher A is broadening her idea of what it looks like to be professional in front of the children. Teacher B is explicitly applying previously unknown mathematical content in her classroom. Teacher C is not only demonstrating remarkable openness by posting this to the blog, she is also demonstrating that she is within her purview to openly question Dr. Ma's views regarding a particular lesson they analyzed together.

EFFECTS

One teacher proclaimed early on, "I didn't know what I didn't know!" Usually teachers enter the elementary classroom with the ability to "do" the work they assign to children. However, the task is, of course, a greater one than that. Skilled elementary math teachers require an unusual perspective on things such as the mathematical underpinning of one example or model versus another, and so forth. To re-explain a concept to a confused child takes diagnostic sophistication that rivals any specialized field. The first step in gaining the skill is admitting that, as elementary school teachers, we are rarely oriented to mathematics in a way that is especially useful in the classroom. Compounding the problem is that it is not entirely possible to introduce the most useful knowledge to teachers until they have become familiar with the common misperceptions of elementary school children. Teachers must be directly exposed, in the most professional manner possible, to the vastness of the mathematics that they were *not* taught in order to become teachers.

A 1st-grade teacher wrote us: "I was quick to dismiss confusion with a math concept as a student not being prepared developmentally for it. Now I consider developmental readiness along with many other factors, including whether or not I have been clear in my instruction." This is a description of another highly sophisticated professional stance. At times, we teachers can opt for the convenient explanation regarding a student's struggle rather than the more labor-intensive one. This teacher is openly questioning the quality of her mathematics instruction. Ma and I contend that it is more difficult to communicate with children about a math concept clearly if a teacher's understanding is superficial. Not only that, we found that increased content knowledge among the teachers seems to spur them on to communicate with more precise and consistent mathematical language and models. Here are another teacher's thoughts: "I found that my students seemed to always count the total number of manipulatives in order to find the answer. Even when the problem involved comparing two sets."

This teacher was amused and a bit annoyed that her 1st graders would do nothing other than "count up how many" to solve any and all math problems. Say Susie had 6 apples and Johnny had 4. Even if the question is how many *more* does Susie have, this teacher's students would dutifully get out the blocks to represent the apples and report that the answer is 10. The teacher in this case took a step back and considered that she had given the students an erroneous impression that the way to solve word problems was to find the numbers in the words and add them up. After several sessions working with Ma and myself regarding the numerous meanings of addition and subtraction (combining, increasing, decreasing, comparing, and so forth), the teacher returned to her class with the helpful knowledge that allowed her to compose problems that varied in solving method so that her students would end this overly automatic approach. Happily, she felt compelled to describe this entire dilemma with her colleagues, demonstrating her stance as a learner as well as reinforcing the idea that sharing a professional dilemma about how to teach the mathematics effectively is not an admission of failure but rather a welcomed contribution to the professional discourse.

Yet another teacher related a serious concern: "I need to really be clear with the following grade teachers about what I was and was not able to cover in math." This teacher's openness that she had not covered all the material at her grade level or the state standards is, in our opinion, highly responsible and especially brave. Clearly, fear of judgment from colleagues or administrators prevented her from communicating such information in the past. It is not at all uncommon for teachers to find it impossible to cover all the material. Everybody knows that, but we don't talk about it. This teacher stepped up, but only because the climate of collaboration had been established. She went on to describe that while she failed to cover some of the introductory material about fractions, she had worked to develop a strong and effective approach to word problems that older grade teachers could use with more advanced mathematics. This level of give-and-take among grade levels led to the trading of videos of lessons and tremendous insight shared about what seemed to be especially beneficial to emphasize often and early in the elementary program and also what seemed to best be introduced in the upper elementary grades. To approach this in a team spirit and with a mindset that the mathematics of the 6 years of elementary school is a single course of study, with a single faculty contributing to it, was invigorating and brought the teachers together to discuss, and even to debate, course content.

In a similar tone another teacher noted, "We agreed early on that we will not be afraid to offer suggestions to our colleagues to further the learning of our students. It's so easy to be defensive when discussing your own teaching, but it just doesn't serve any purpose." The atmosphere established at Slater School faculty meetings was that of a laboratory where colleagues urged one another to innovate as well as to share explicitly what they felt were ongoing problems in the classroom. Like laboratory data, students' papers, as well as video clips from the classroom, informed the faculty as to what was actually occurring in the classrooms. Teachers learned how to focus their discussions on solutions that were based on the evidence rather than on a story as told by a teacher. Because teachers had the opportunity to engage in peer observation and to provide feedback in groups of three, the climate of open feedback emerged with the larger grade-level faculty group and with the entire faculty. Liping Ma demonstrating her teaching both live and in video also supported this climate early in the program. After these sessions, Ma was quick to encourage the teachers to offer their thoughts about what was problematic about her teaching. Her humility and humor shone through on these occasions. She, as a renowned scholar, had managed to make it clear that she was at a loss of how to really contribute to this particular school without the expertise of the teachers who know the children.

This last point is a very important one. The leader of a professional development effort is allowed *not* to know everything. In fact, it is especially important that he or she demonstrate humility regarding the content and context at hand and to model his or her own arc of learning within the effort.

COLLABORATION REDEFINED AT SLATER SCHOOL

In brief, a profound shift happened at Slater School as a result of the teachers' in-depth work with mathematics content. They discarded an earlier notion that the purpose of collaboration was to make the work of teaching easier. Instead, they grew to view collaboration as an ongoing commitment to make the teaching at the school *better*. Teachers also became skeptical of longtime practices they had previously deemed successful. They stopped asking what the kids "did" during math time and instead asked what the kids "learned." Capitalizing on elements of Lesson Study type professional development, triads of teachers at the same grade level established a trusting relationship devoted to improvement. The effects of such relationships permeated the entire grade level and, in time, the entire faculty. Faculty meetings became learning environments not unlike the classrooms with similar norms to support learning. Teachers described it as "rigor with support." They engaged in discourse rather than limiting themselves to exchanges of opinions. Their collaboration placed teacher learning squarely and openly on the school's larger agenda. Coherence regarding instructional approaches, conceptual relationships in mathematics, and questions regarding grade-level emphasis all were commonly discussed both formally within meetings and informally among teachers throughout the course of the day. Specific markers that Ma and I noticed that we could directly link to the faculty's development as a community of learners are the following:

1. Teachers were motivated to analyze student misunderstandings so that they could bring a learning dilemma to their colleagues as a case to address together. They often collected evidence (student work, awkwardly worded materials, and so forth) for colleagues' review.
2. Teachers made more thoughtful decisions in their own classrooms following collaboration opportunities. Often these were proactive choices based on the confusion encountered by students in a colleague's classroom.
3. With more developed math content knowledge, teachers had more thorough and mathematically accurate conversations with students and with one another.
4. Teachers learned to relate math concepts and took their sequence of instruction more seriously. They were no longer hesitant to request meetings with teachers of higher and lower grade levels so that they could reach agreement on mathematical language, support English language learners, and review issues of assessment.
5. Most important, teachers looked anew at the choices they once considered beyond question. On her website, Brenda Wallace (2007), a professional developer in literacy, puts it well: "Much of the work of professional development is to lift people up and engage in a process of change, moving from a stance of certainty to curiosity" (np).

CHALLENGES

Now that the project is complete, Liping Ma and I have looked back to notice a number of challenges that we are confident those with greater experience in professional development will address. First of all, how can a school use site-specific data and at the same time align to a course of study that develops mathematical knowledge for teaching? Also, how can we constructively challenge the "activity mindset" so prevalent in schools? This is not to say that activities are bad. The point is that math activities often are developed for reasons other than to promote the learning of anything specific. How can teachers be encouraged to use their understanding of developmental readiness to increase learning rather than as a reason to back away from a rigorous task? How can teachers be supported in dealing with the highly idiosyncratic methods of assessments mandated by various levels of a district and by federal law and not be drawn into test-driven teaching? How can schools communicate the nature of content-based professional development to the parents of a school community, assuring them the approaches used with their children are not faddish and the teachers at the site are not learning math that they should "already" know?

The stigma associated with undeveloped math content knowledge among teachers is debilitating. The teachers at Slater Elementary were able to move through periods of embarrassment to later make comments such as: "I just never knew this stuff" and "I hated math. I was totally humiliated in high school." Professional development facilitators in math all understand this dynamic among elementary teachers, yet we also understand how critical it is that we repair the damage.

8

Understanding Science: The Role of Community in Content Learning

Mayumi Shinohara
Kirsten B. Daehler

Zadie King is confused. Today is the first of eight meetings of her science study group, which meets after school in the classroom of one of the teachers in the group. Zadie and her colleagues (15 teachers in all, including Rosa, the group's facilitator) decided to study electric circuits, the topic of a kit-based unit in their district's 4th-grade curriculum. Everyone wants to learn more science, which is why the group decided to focus on content. Most teachers agree that the unit on circuits is the most difficult science unit of the year, though their reasons vary. Some teachers find the hands-on activities challenging to lead. Others feel unclear about the point of the unit. Still others find the unit intimidating and admit they have never taught it. Zadie has taught the unit twice. She notices that students love the hands-on activities but don't seem to emerge with a better understanding of the big ideas. She speaks for many in the group when she says, "I feel like it's my fault. If I just understood the science better, my students would learn a lot more."

When the group decided on its focus, teachers talked about *what* they wanted to learn and *how*. One teacher said, "I want to do the hands-on activities and talk about what they're supposed to help students learn." Another teacher talked about what to avoid: "What I don't need is another lecture about stuff that isn't related to what we teach kids. To be honest, I don't want a lecture, period." The group also considered a variety of science resources. Rosa recommended a course she experienced as a member of the district's science leadership team: "It really opened my eyes to what it means to learn content. I even took a follow-up course on facilitation." While Rosa suggested the course, it was the group that ultimately made the decision. What appealed to Zadie about the course was its focus on science and professional community.

Rosa began the first meeting by sharing a set of group norms.

> Our goal is to learn science, so we'll be doing a lot of thinking and talking about evidence. It's helpful to share your ideas openly, even if you don't understand them completely yourself or if you think they might be wrong. Thinking things through together and learning from one another's ideas, correct and incorrect, are important parts of community learning and will help us get more out of our time. You'll notice that I won't give you the right answer or serve as the group expert. This doesn't mean I don't know or that I'm trying to torture you. It means I'm making room for you to do the thinking. My job is to guide our learning by keeping the discussion grounded in evidence, prompting people to fully explain their ideas, and asking for alternative ideas and points of view.

Zadie finds these norms confusing. She wonders,

> How am I supposed to learn if Rosa doesn't tell me the right answer? She's the expert. I'm here to learn. What can I contribute to other people's learning if I don't feel solid in the content myself?

Zadie is also anxious about being wrong in front of her peers. She knows she is no science expert, yet Zadie feels guilty that she doesn't have a better understanding of what she is teaching her students. The course Zadie and her peers are experiencing (Daehler & Shinohara, in press) was developed by our project, Understanding Science. The questions she raises exemplify the confusion teachers commonly feel when they first encounter unfamiliar elements of our approach to learning science.

The fundamental goal of Understanding Science is to improve the science achievement of K–8 students, especially English learners and students with poor literacy skills, by building the content knowledge and pedagogical content knowledge of their teachers. Since 1998, we have worked with more than 1,000 teachers in 20 states, impacting an estimated 18,000 students. Understanding Science courses positively impact both teacher knowledge and student achievement (Heller, 2006). An especially encouraging result is that low-performing students make the biggest gains.

Our work draws heavily on current ideas about learning in professional communities, but does so for the purpose of developing teachers' disciplinary knowledge of content and pedagogy, not just their instructional practices. Understanding Science courses address three salient challenges: (1) helping teachers learn how to learn science through a collaborative, social process, (2) creating an environment within which teachers rigorously explore the meaning of science ideas, and (3) balancing teacher attention to content and pedagogy.

This chapter explores the role of community in our efforts to help teachers learn both science and science for teaching. In doing so, it illustrates how we address the challenges above and describes the design of our professional development, along with evaluation results and lessons learned.

DESIGN OF OUR PROFESSIONAL DEVELOPMENT

The focus of the Understanding Science approach is the intersection of knowledge about content and teaching—that is, on developing teachers' pedagogical content knowledge. The model is based on the premise that, to develop pedagogical content knowledge, teachers must have opportunities to learn *science content knowledge* in combination with an *analysis of student thinking* about that content and *instructional strategies* for helping students learn that content (Shinohara, Daehler, & Heller, 2004; Shymansky & Matthews, 1993; Van Driel, Verloop, & Wallace, 2007). Narrative cases, drawn from actual classroom episodes, bring together science content, student thinking, and instruction. The case materials are written by classroom teachers under the guidance of project staff, and contain student work, dialogue, descriptions of instructional materials, and activities, along with examples of teacher thinking and behavior.

The logic model motivating this approach (see Figure 8.1) describes the cascade of influences connecting teachers' experiences in Understanding Science courses to student outcomes. The theory of action underlying the approach posits that when the professional development is situated in an environment of collaborative, professional inquiry—one that is rich in talk about scientific meanings in conjunction with a focus on student thinking and critical analysis of practice—this leads to increases in teachers' science content and pedagogical content knowledge. These outcomes for teachers, in turn, result in changes in classroom practices, such as increased accuracy of science representations and explanations, a focus on conceptual understanding and academic language development, and opportunities for students to talk to learn science. Classroom changes ultimately produce improvements in student achievement along with increased development of all students' academic language in science and reduced achievement gaps for low-performing students and English learners.

Each course focuses on a different topic and grade span (for example, rocks and minerals for grades 3–5, force and motion for grades 6–8) and offers 24 hours of professional development, divided into eight 3-hour sessions and sequenced such that science ideas build and grow over time. Courses are correlated to the National Science Education Standards for easy use with any standards-based science curriculum. At present, the program consists of six content courses for teachers: two for elementary and four for middle school. Ultimately, the full set of Understanding Science courses will present a coherent professional development curriculum, including 15 courses on the major ideas of K–8 earth, life, and physical science.

Figure 8.1. *Understanding the Science Logic Model.* Links between intended outcomes and features of the professional development are shown.

Professional Development Features	Teacher Outcomes	Classroom Outcomes	Student Outcomes
Exploration of science ideas	Knowledge of science content	Science taught accurately	Improved science achievement
Exploration of science language	Pedagogical content knowledge	Focus on developing conceptual understanding	Improved science academic language
Focus on student thinking	Strategies for building students' academic language	Focus on developing academic language	
Critical analysis of practice	Belief in the value of classroom science talk	Opportunities to talk to learn science	Reduced achievement gap for English learners

Understanding Science courses are used in a variety of settings. While intentionally designed for use in existing professional development programs, such as ongoing study groups or summer institutes that support standards-based instruction and implementation of science curricula, existing materials are found as the central focus of university master's programs for science teachers and as the "sense-making" part of pre-service science methods courses.

MATERIALS FOR TEACHERS AND STAFF DEVELOPERS

Materials for each course are presented in a set of two books: a casebook for teachers and a facilitator guide for staff developers.

Casebooks contain eight chapters (one per session) and present the materials teachers need to participate in all eight sessions of a professional development course. Each chapter contains a teaching case of actual classroom practice that illustrates students' science thinking and highlights an important teaching dilemma that any teacher might face, along with a companion content guide that explains and illustrates core science concepts.

Facilitator guides also contain eight core chapters (one per session) and provide extensive support materials and detailed procedures needed to successfully lead a course. Each chapter describes the underlying science (including common misconceptions of children and adults) and provides scripted yet flexible procedures, such as instructions to guide the hands-on and sense-making work in each science investigation, guiding questions for each case discussion, and instructions for completing the classroom connection assignment teachers do between sessions. For ease of use, the facilitator guides also include: goals, syllabus, required materials and preparation, and blackline masters of all handouts and charts.

Supporting chapters in the facilitator guide share lessons learned from the experiences of staff developers across the country. They also address logistical issues inherent in organizing and leading a course. For example, they offer practical suggestions for adapting the course to different formats and audiences, help staff developers know what up-front preparation is necessary (such as intellectual preparation, gathering and organizing materials, room arrangements), and recommend roles and responsibilities for solo- and co-facilitation.

LEARNING TO LEARN SCIENCE TOGETHER

A primary challenge of our work is to help teachers learn how to learn science together through collaborative social interaction. This challenge comes up when the experiences (and therefore the beliefs) of K–8 teachers are fundamentally at odds with conceptions of the nature of science, and therefore what is widely considered to be the best instructional practice. Science learning is largely about the production and interpretation of evidence. It involves the social construction of knowledge and, at times, incorrect ideas. In contrast, most K–8 teachers learned science by reading a textbook, spitting back correct answers, and occasionally conducting a lab to confirm some fact or formula. As a result, they have come to know science as a domain of facts and right answers. It can be very challenging for them to share tentative thinking, ground their ideas in evidence, or go through periods of uncertainty or disequilibrium. Even teachers who support hands-on science or inquiry for students may be inclined to say, "Just give me the answer" or "Tell me the right way to do it."

So, in our courses, we assume it is important to raise fundamental questions about the nature of science and science learning, and to explicitly support teachers in learning science through collaborative, evidence-based discussions. One way we do this is through the negotiation of specific norms for group interaction, as well as clear and specific roles and responsibilities for teacher learners and for the facilitator. Another way we support teachers in learning to learn science together is by carefully scaffolding their learning so teachers have opportunities to gradually take on their roles and refine ideas and skills.

For example, the following vignette illustrates how we help teachers refine their science ideas and practice their science thinking and talking skills.
The vignette captures a science investigation, held during the second meeting
of Zadie's science study group.

> The topic of the second meeting is electrical current and series circuits (circuits
> where current can travel in just one pathway or in a continuous loop). Guided by
> a science investigation handout, Zadie works with two other peers to build series
> circuits, investigate bulb brightness and current, and learn to represent current
> with arrows and lines. After roughly 40 minutes, Rosa brings everyone together
> for a whole-group discussion of the science. She begins by inviting groups to
> each share one comparison or claim from their hands-on work:
>
> > *Draw a pair of circuits that surprised you or helped you learn something.*
> > *Explain what you found surprising or what your circuits helped you learn.*
>
> Teachers draw their circuits on half-sheets of paper and Rosa asks them to
> place each circuit according to the brightness of its bulbs onto a graphic orga-
> nizer. The organizer, which is an arrow, serves as a continuum for comparing and
> ordering the brightness of bulbs and, therefore, the current in the circuits.
>
> Because teachers have mucked around with circuits in small groups, most
> find it easy to join the discussion and add something substantive and unique
> (e.g., "Three bulbs are dimmer than two, two bulbs are dimmer than one," and
> "Adding batteries makes the bulb brighter"). Zadie appreciates that the initial
> discussion is low-risk, safe, and inclusive. She listens carefully to what other
> teachers say and jots down ideas, phrases, and evidence she finds helpful.
>
> Once teachers have talked about and compared several pairs of circuits,
> Rosa turns the group's attention to more general, conventionally scientific pat-
> terns in the data by asking: "What factors seem to affect the current?"
>
> Having an ordered set of circuit drawings to look at, front and center, makes
> it easy for Zadie to notice and talk about patterns in the evidence and to follow
> what other people say. However, the shared data set by no means ensures that
> she (or other teachers) get everything right the first time. At first, some teach-
> ers incorrectly believe the brightness of the bulb is solely determined by the
> number of batteries in the circuit. Other teachers mistakenly think it's all about
> the number of bulbs. The group tests each idea in turn, moving and regrouping
> the circuit drawings on the board to illustrate and evaluate ideas. Rosa prompts
> teachers to more fully explain their ideas by asking, "Can you say more about
> that?" and "What makes you think so?" Equally important, she turns their at-
> tention to facts, definitions, or evidence that teachers have forgotten or glossed

over by asking focusing questions about the hands-on activity or content notes teachers read prior to the meeting.

It is the fact that bulb brightness is the same in circuits with equal numbers of batteries and bulbs (e.g., one battery and one bulb, two batteries and two bulbs, and three batteries and three bulbs) that helps Zadie and the group see that the numbers of both the batteries and the bulbs matter. In fact, it is the ratio of the number of batteries to the number of bulbs that determines the brightness of bulbs (and therefore current) in a series circuit.

SCAFFOLDING TEACHER LEARNING

Notice that Zadie experiences three opportunities to refine her ideas and practice her science thinking and talking skills: first in a group of three when she builds circuits and talks about them informally (and at times tentatively) with peers; next with the whole class when teachers compare and sequence bulb brightness (current) in pairs of circuits; and third with the whole class when teachers discuss the factors that influence current. Each opportunity gives Zadie a chance to practice the skill of comparison with an increasingly larger and more abstractly represented set of circuits (first pairs of circuits, then a collection of 10–15 circuits the group has posted; first actual circuits, then drawings) and to do so more and more publicly. Thus, each learning opportunity prepares her for the next, allowing her to gradually learn how to learn science with others and take on the mantle of an accomplished science learner. By the third opportunity, teachers have efficiently built the knowledge, skills, and confidence needed to tackle a core science concept (the factors affecting current in a series circuit), one that is prominent in national and state standards and valued by the scientific community.

NORMS FOR GROUP DISCUSSION

In the vignette above, it is Rosa, the facilitator, who keeps the group discussion grounded in evidence and prompts teachers to fully explain their science ideas (e.g., by sharing a claim, coupled with the evidence and reasoning that led to it). She guides the discussion by asking questions rather than explaining the science. Over the course of the eight meetings, the group will take on these responsibilities, but for now, they are learning to listen carefully to and consider one another's ideas. Understandably, most find it easier to objectively evaluate the ideas of others than their own. By practicing the skill of evidence-based thinking and talking in a community, teachers gradually internalize the norms and standards of science and learn to learn science together.

EXPLORING THE MEANING OF SCIENCE IDEAS

A second challenge is to rigorously explore the meaning of science ideas. Based on their prior experience, an overwhelming number of K–8 teachers think of science as a collection of dusty facts or formulas. To them, understanding science ideas means memorization or "plugging and chugging" numbers into formulas. These beliefs trip teachers up when they try to teach science through inquiry and discussion. After all, what is there to really inquire about or discuss?

So in our courses, we try to illustrate that science is an interpretive process and that the same evidence or idea can be construed in many different yet correct ways. One way we help groups go beyond a surface understanding of science ideas and grapple with other, less obvious meanings is to ask teachers to make their thinking visible by sharing it with the group, even if their ideas are not yet fully clear in their minds. Each contribution helps the group deepen its understanding of science ideas. We also prompt groups to reflect on their own learning process and that of others, for example by asking, "What parts were difficult? Where did the ah-ha's come? What were the cognitive steps and challenges?"

In the previous vignette, Zadie and her group discovered a central concept of circuits known as Ohm's Law by *qualitatively* describing the relationships among current (the brightness of bulbs in a circuit), voltage (the number of batteries), and resistance (the number of bulbs). Over the next few meetings, they will unpack the meaning of Ohm's Law by revisiting it several times and sharing alternative ways of thinking about what it represents or helps them understand about circuits.

For example, they will develop a more formal understanding of each variable and learn how to *quantify* the relationships among them in a single equation. While not developmentally appropriate for elementary students, Ohm's Law is a useful way for teachers to think about the relationships among current (I), voltage (V), and resistance (R) in a circuit: $V = I \times R$.

When groups encounter the formula for Ohm's Law, it is common for teachers to share strong, sometimes opposing reactions. Some teachers love the precision of the formula. Others may resist making quantitative comparisons due to their varying degrees of comfort with mathematics. Either way, few come to see and appreciate the real implications of the law merely by examining its mathematical formulation.

Having the chance to unpack Ohm's Law in terms of both words and mathematical expressions helps many teachers recognize and revise their own common yet incorrect ideas, especially about current and voltage. For example, at first many mistakenly believe batteries always generate the same current, when in fact batteries generate different current from circuit to circuit. This point can drive home an important distinction: current and voltage are not the same thing. This idea may seem obvious, given the formula for Ohm's

Law. Yet it is an idea that eludes many until it crops up several times and for several people. Initially, groups may be surprised to learn that some incorrect ideas come up again and again. But, upon listening to the ideas of others, they come to realize that incorrect ideas can have a logic of their own, though that logic is typically based on more limited information or evidence. For example, it's easy to assume a battery has a set "strength," in part as a result of batteries being identified in our everyday world by their voltage (for example, 1.5 volts or 6 volts). Thus it is only natural, yet incorrect, to equate "strength" with current, which leads us to incorrectly conclude that the same battery always generates the same current, and the same current means the same light.

When teachers share different reactions to Ohm's Law, the entire group comes to value the merits of different ways of understanding science ideas while appreciating their pros and cons. Everyone benefits by hearing the ideas and experiences of others. As teachers explore the meaning of Ohm's Law in different ways and through different perspectives, they construct a richer, deeper, more accurate understanding of its meaning, one that prepares them to effectively teach circuits to their students.

BALANCING CONTENT AND PEDAGOGY

A third challenge is to achieve a balance of group attention to both content and pedagogy. It is tempting for groups of teachers to retreat from the discomfort of learning science content to more familiar topics, such as instructional strategies or activities. Some science workshops avoid this pitfall by dealing with content alone, cleansed of all reference to students and teaching. A deep understanding of science is essential but not sufficient for effective teaching. Teachers must also know "how to organize, sequence, and present the content to cater to the diverse interests and abilities of the students" (Barnett & Hodson, 2001, p. 432). In short, what teachers need is pedagogical content knowledge.

What is unique about the teaching process is that it requires teachers to "transform" their subject matter knowledge for the purpose of teaching. This transformation occurs as the teacher critically reflects on and interprets the subject matter; finds multiple ways to represent the information as analogies, metaphors, examples, problems, demonstrations, and/or classroom activities; adapts the material to students' developmental levels and abilities, gender, prior knowledge, and misconceptions; and finally *tailors* the material to those whom the information will be taught (Shulman, 1986).

In our courses, we use teaching cases to raise fundamental questions of content yet situate them in the context of real students and classrooms, thus promoting a balance between content and pedagogy. The following vignette illustrates what a typical case discussion looks like. As you read the vignette, notice how the discussion is peppered with content, even when teachers are discussing student thinking and teaching. Also notice how teachers are again encouraged to share their thinking, thus adding to the rigor of the discussion.

> Following the science investigation, teachers examine student thinking in groups of three and critically analyze instruction presented in the case. Rosa asks one or two groups to say a little about their discussion of one student's thinking: "What does Hannah understand about current? What is she missing? What does Hannah think happens to current when it reaches a bulb?" Rosa makes a public record of teachers' ideas by writing on large charts of the student's work, designating correct and incorrect student thinking with different colors and encouraging people with different ideas to speak, asking, "What is another interpretation? Does anyone have a different way of thinking about that?"
>
> The discussion of student work naturally leads to a discussion of the instruction in the case, specifically an activity involving passing ping-pong balls that the teacher in the case used to help students understand current. By now, teachers mostly agree on what students should know about current and what is hard for students to understand. Their discussions become more heated when they try to figure out what contributed to students' inaccurate ways of thinking and what to do about it.
>
> Some teachers blame the ping-pong ball model for Hannah's difficulties because it doesn't help students understand what happens to current in bulbs. Others think the ping-pong ball model is a great way to help children understand that current flows in one direction, in a continuous loop, and in varying amounts (thus explaining brighter and dimmer bulbs). These teachers can't fathom why students incorrectly show current coming out of both ends of the battery or describe bulbs as "using it up," because the models are so concrete and clear. Still other teachers are convinced by their own experience during the science investigation and think that if the teacher had started with a necklace model this would have solved everything. But would it?

Notice how looking at student work helps the group solidify their understanding of the science while at the same time pointing out the ways in which students commonly think about and misunderstand current in series circuits. When teachers first read the case, prior to the meeting, many share the incorrect ideas of students in the case, namely that current is "shared" or "used up" by the bulbs, rather than flowing in a continuous loop from one end of the battery to the other.

Also notice in the vignette above how the group's analysis of teaching integrates their newfound understanding of both science and student thinking. By discussing the teacher's choice of the ping-pong model to demonstrate current in a circuit, the group evaluates how well the model matches what students are struggling to understand. With Rosa's guidance, the group weighs the pros and cons of various instructional choices. This leads teachers to explore alternative perspectives and solutions, which in turn causes them to rethink their instruction even as they deepen their content knowledge.

EVALUATION RESULTS AND LESSONS LEARNED

In navigating the challenges above, we have been lucky to work with many outstanding teachers, teacher educators, scientists, and researchers. Below are some of the lessons we have learned with (and from) them about the role of community in content learning.

One lesson learned is that professional communities can learn challenging science, and gain insight into the learning of science, by examining evidence and openly and deeply exploring their own understandings. An extensive, multiyear study (Heller, 2006) showed that Understanding Science courses positively impact both teacher knowledge and student achievement:

- Students of all entering abilities showed significant gains in science.
- Teachers learned science, developed more sophisticated pedagogical content knowledge, and maintained these gains over time.
- Teachers reported changes in their classroom practice in general, not only for course topics they studied. They also became clearer as to what students should know and were more discriminating about what students were actually learning.

In fact, teachers are typically far more skilled at learning science than they (and sometimes the teacher educators and scientists who work with them) realize. Science is fundamentally a form of logic that is applied to making sense of the world. And logic is something most adults, and therefore teachers, are very good at, since it is a skill we practice and use every day. So when teachers learn to use logic, comparison, and other everyday skills to unpack science ideas, many are happy to learn that science is not as difficult or mysterious as it seems. They also learn that prior knowledge is not the same thing as skill. This in turn gives them the confidence they need to broaden and refine their skills and to adopt disciplinary norms, standards, and perspectives.

Another lesson learned is that professional communities can play a vital role in the development of teachers' science thinking and talking skills. When teachers first learn to learn science, many find it difficult to objectively evaluate their ideas against evidence. This is where community-based learning kicks in. When the "rules" for evaluating science ideas are made clear to all (i.e., they need to come from and be supported by all of the known evidence), the community can evaluate one another's ideas, freeing teachers up to share tentative thinking and put its trust in the group. (More people, more observations and evidence, more accuracy.) This involves teachers in evaluating the ideas of others and gives them important opportunities to practice their science thinking and talking skills. Learning science with others also exposes teachers to a wider variety of interpretations and ways of thinking, allowing them to more fully explore and understand the meaning of science ideas.

A third lesson learned deals with the development of pedagogical content knowledge in science. While professional communities may begin with a more limited understanding of science, they clearly bring significant resources and expertise about students and teaching. So we have found it highly advantageous to combine opportunities for teachers to learn science with opportunities to analyze teaching, so they develop a deeply intertwined knowledge of both content and pedagogical content.

A fourth lesson learned is that increasing the role of community in science learning does not diminish (much less eliminate) the role of leaders. To support the learning of science and of science for teaching in professional communities, leaders must have an even deeper knowledge of science content and exemplary approaches to science teaching (i.e., hands-on investigation, inquiry, and social construction of knowledge).

It is worth noting that these lessons learned emerged from a community of practice, not the solitary musings of any one person. Over the years, we have made important progress, but we continue to work on the challenges that inevitably crop up when teachers make sense of science through collaborative social interaction. Our work with Understanding Science continues to teach us about the role of community in content learning, just as it does for teachers.

Reflecting on the Themes of Context, Commitment, Capacity, Content, and Challenge

Ann Lieberman
Lynne Miller

The themes of context, commitment, capacity, content, and challenge cut across the five cases presented in the previous chapters. These themes serve as lenses though which we can understand how teachers come together and how they learn to simultaneously build teaching competence and professional community. In addition, the cases provide real-life responses to the questions that we posed at the beginning of this volume: What difference does context make? Why does context matter? How do communities build commitment from their members? What kind of commitments do members make? How do members develop the capacity to collaborate with and learn from each other? What new capacities do groups build in their members? How do communities deal with the competing agendas of content and process issues? What happens when they do not? And last, what common challenges emerge from these separate narratives of professional communities? We consider each of the themes separately as they apply to the cases and introduce each one with excerpts about what we had learned about the theme from our review of research and development in Part One.

THE CONTEXTS

Context matters. Factors such as where a community is located, the culture that surrounds it, the way it gets started, and its conditions of membership combine to impact the trajectories it takes and the challenges it faces.

When the project directors wrote about their individual contexts, they described the participants, the institutions where they worked, the purposes of their projects, and where and how they began. For example, Ellinger described Slater Elementary School, where he and Liping Ma were invited to help teachers improve their math teaching. The teachers had already scheduled weekly grade-level meetings and hoped that, in the process of planning together and having peers observe and review student work, they would deepen their understanding of the mathematics content and how to teach it. In this context, collaboration of a sort was already a part of the school ethos; there were structures and expectations in place that allowed teachers to meet regularly and engage in group work. The principal had encouraged the kindergarten and 1st-grade teachers to participate, as well. In effect, the context exhibited a readiness to begin the math project before the project directors even arrived.

The context that Cziko described in the MUSE credential program at Berkeley, where she was responsible for teaching pre-service English teachers how to work in multicultural settings, was quite different. She entered a setting that was overloaded with expectations, where students had very little time to learn a great deal. In only 1½ years, they enrolled in two graduate courses, participated in a 1-week intensive writing workshop that was followed by 20 hours of student teaching, and then enrolled in an additional four courses. Cziko, who had been a successful secondary teacher for years, assumed that she could help her students best by sharing with them what she had found helpful in her own experience in multicultural settings. Community building seemed like an "extra," something that might be added on but was not a central part of how she would construct the time students spent together. She soon discovered that her initial ideas about teaching through apprenticeship, inquiry, and collaboration were in conflict with the expectations of her students. Recognizing the tension between her goals for the students and their expressed needs, she saw her ideas fall into the dust bin and quickly learned that the context demanded that she build community first, that it was a prerequisite to building competence. Without a context that established norms of trust, openness, and honest talk, the pre-service teachers were not inclined to disclose publicly the issues they faced in their own learning and teaching.

In their description of New Teacher Center program (NTC), Moir and Hanson identified another situation where the goals that the director held for students were not in line with the needs that the students brought to the table. Moir and her staff responded by assigning a mentor to each new teacher for his or her first 2 years on the job. The quality of the mentor–teacher relationship, "built on trust, looking for entry points, and helping teachers to reflect on their pedagogical practices to build their competence," became the hallmark of the project for novice teachers.

However, Moir soon realized that she needed something equally compelling for the mentors, something that would increase their understanding of and competence in their new roles. The Mentor Forum was born, and it became a new context for teacher learning. From its beginning, the Forum was designed thoughtfully to provide a setting that would help illuminate the knowledge and skills that the mentors had developed over time and that new teachers needed to learn. It became a place where the mentors could not only identify ways they could help new teachers learn on the job, but also served as a venue where they could go more deeply into their craft as teachers. As a result, the mentors became consciously engaged in their own learning, in a way similar to how the novice teachers were engaged. In this case, a newly created Mentor Forum changed the context of the New Teacher Center.

These three cases demonstrate how different contexts present different demands and require different responses on the part of project leaders. In Ellinger's case, the context that he and Liping Ma entered at Slater Elementary had collaborative norms in place. This gave them a starting point from which they could introduce what they called "Lesson Study Lite" in mathematics to teachers. Cziko's case was decidedly different. The MUSE program, with its packed agenda and limited time, had no existing collaborative structures to frame the work; Cziko had to create them. She realized that building trust and a sense of community needed to come first. Similarly, Moir realized that, in addition to creating a professional community for novice teachers, she also had to create a new context for the professional learning of the mentors.

DEVELOPING COMMITMENTS

Commitments take time to develop; there is no such thing as an instant community. Members have to get to know one another and build norms of trust before they can commit to the process of learning from one another.

The stories that the project directors tell provide compelling evidence that, as people join a community and become involved in its work, they begin to feel differently about themselves, about their peers, and about their own learning. They gradually commit to learning from one another and to new identities as community members.

Cziko involved her students in a variety of activities that were designed to build trust and community; this helped her students open up to new processes and content. The students introduced themselves to their colleagues, went on a field trip together, and wrote about their experiences. After Cziko provided opportunities for students to *learn about* one another, she helped them learn how to *learn from* one another and to understand what it means to be part of a professional community. She arranged workshops that unlocked ideas for writing, beginning with writing letters to the cooperating teachers. She arranged other activities that were geared toward building trust and commitment on the part of group members both to one another and to the process of learning what it takes to be a teacher. In time, the students gained confidence in tackling the tougher parts of being a teacher. They came to understand that they were part of a community of colleagues where they could safely share their growing understandings and their confusions about teaching, and they discovered that they could learn from and with one another. The students demonstrated their developing commitment to the community as they began to arrange social and academic events for themselves and spent "hours teaching and learning from one another over dozens of cups of coffee at the local cafe."

Ellinger and Liping Ma forged commitment in another way. Unlike Cziko, they did not work with teachers every day, nor did they have the opportunity to craft a culture from the beginning. Because they came into the school from the outside and intervened in the day-to-day work of teachers, they had to work hard to develop a community of math teachers who were committed to building a professional community and, at the same time, were committed to building competence and confidence in the content and pedagogies of mathematics. They had to develop trust and credibility before they could engage teachers in an examination of math and how they taught it. Ellinger began by teaching classes to students and having the lessons videotaped. By disclosing his own teaching to the community members, he began the process of building a climate that honored open discussion about pedagogy. This led to deeper investigations and uncovered common misconceptions about math and math teaching. The teachers invested more of themselves as they watched one another teach, learned how to provide feedback that was direct and not merely complimentary, and grappled with the complexity of understanding and teaching mathematics.

Commitment to the idea of being part of the community developed over time. The teachers became familiar with a five-step problem-solving approach that helped structure their conversations: (1) understand the question; (2) record the data; (3) develop a plan; (4) formulate an answer; and (5) check the answer. As competence with the procedure developed, so did dedication to the process. Similarly, when teachers learned the elements of Lesson Study and engaged with an area of math that was tough to teach, they became skilled in a cycle of planning, observing, and debriefing. They worked in groups of three to plan a lesson and decide who would teach it, and they met afterward to discuss how the lesson went and whether it achieved its objectives. As routines of practice and reflection took hold, teachers dug deeply into their emerging understandings of "fundamental math" and became energized by their own learning, going so far as to create a blog where they posed questions, concerns, comments, and compliments. The project directors had managed to build momentum and a commitment to learning math content and improving math pedagogy that was strengthened through collaboration and community membership.

In the Moir and Hanson case, the Mentor Forum was the vehicle through which commitment was fashioned. The Forum met weekly for 3 hours at a time and was based on a curriculum that included a variety of tools to help new teachers examine their practice, analyze student work, engage in active listening, analyze teacher performance based on standards, and assess mentor growth and development. Along with the curriculum, the Forum established connecting activities, problem-posing and problem-solving situations, time for sharing a current problem or dilemma, opportunities for reflection and feedback, and ways to plan for future Forums. The mentors owned the conversations, working together as partners and taking turns in setting the agenda. The structure of the Forum engaged mentors with one another in the same way that novice teachers were engaged with their mentors. As they worked together, the mentors became committed to one another and to the process of their own learning.

BUILDING CAPACITY

The capacity of members to engage fully in teaching communities grows as commitments develop. They learn how to talk together honestly, to engage in knowledge work both as producers and critical consumers of new theories and ideas, and to make connections between their own learning, their teaching practices, and the impact these have on students. They begin to see themselves and act differently; they reinvent themselves as teachers and reinvigorate their careers.

The cases demonstrated how the various projects built the capacity of members to learn from one another, to collaborate, to take responsibility for one another, and to participate fully in shared purposes. Although many teachers came to the projects, networks, and reform groups with little or no experience in collaboration, they learned new skills and habits as a result of their engagement in teaching communities.

Pointer Mace's narrative described three teachers who were involved in creating multimedia records of their teaching practice, a relatively new idea with significant teaching and learning potential. By recording what they believed, how they thought about their students, and what they did in their classrooms, the teachers developed new capacities. They not only learned how to engage in deep content work, they also learned how to connect their own learning to classroom practice and how to place their work on public display for a wide audience. In doing so, they came to see themselves as more than classroom teachers: They assumed roles as leaders in instruction and professional development and as competent media designers.

Shinohara and Daehler provided ways for science teachers to build their capacities through joint inquiry into narrative cases that described "classic science dilemmas." The cases invited teachers to identify with the problems, collaborate in discovering ways to solve them, expand their own repertoire, and connect their professional learning to their classroom practice. As they looked at student work and science dilemmas that were authentic, complex, and universal, the teachers learned how to engage in honest talk about issues of teaching and content; they came to openly share what they would do in similar situations and how they would work with their students. The case materials, coupled with facilitation by someone who knew science well, provided teachers with clear direction within a community of peers and increased their capacity as teachers and learners of science.

Cziko's approach to capacity building was to construct a series of activities that were designed to model for pre-service teachers what it means to be a member of a professional community. The activities engaged students in learning about themselves and about one another. Through a sequence that began with introductions and storytelling and moved on to partnering and extensions into the larger community, Cziko laid the foundation for the development of trusting and open conversations and the free exchange of ideas as well as for a shared stance of inquiry and reflection. All of this led to new understandings by the pre-service teachers about the communities they would eventually serve and the professional community of which they had become a part.

These three examples illustrate the diverse ways that projects created opportunities for participants to build their capacity as competent teachers and as engaged community members. Such capacity building did not just happen. It was thoughtfully developed over time and connected people in a common struggle to know more about their subject matter, to connect their professional learning to their individual classroom practice, and to engage students in the bettering of their own lives. In the cases we examined, materials, products, and structured activities engaged teachers in honest talk, invited them to publicly disclose the complexities they encountered in their practice, and helped them develop strategies for particular student populations and discover new knowledge about their craft.

BALANCING CONTENT AND PROCESS

Content matters, but it has to be balanced with process. Communities grapple with the problem of how to deepen subject matter knowledge and content-related pedagogies while, at the same time, being mindful of the processes that keep the community alive and strong. While it is impossible to keep the balance all of the time, communities need to guard against going too far in either direction.

Each of the cases placed content firmly on its agenda, and each saw the need to balance it with process. While Moir and Hanson recognized that mentors need to develop content knowledge about how to mentor novice teachers, they also acknowledged that this would not happen in a vacuum. They created the Mentor Forum as a community where accomplished teachers could help one another increase their knowledge about teaching in general and mentoring in particular. Members investigated teaching problems, examined the complexity of mentor–mentee relationships, and considered strategies for working with novice teachers. In the process, they deepened their content knowledge about the very act of teaching at the same time that they developed processes of community building that sustained their collaborative intellectual and practical work.

In Ellinger's case, content was primary; and while the content was clearly mathematics, it was a particular view of math. Working with Liping Ma, Ellinger wanted teachers to understand the difference between *basic* and *fundamental* math. He defined *basic math* as a collection of procedures. *Fundamental math* was more complex, having three components: (1) elementary math, the beginning of the discipline; (2) primary math, the rudiments of advanced mathematics; and (3) foundational math, which supports future learning. Ma realized that she could not approach the math agenda without attending to process and took it upon herself to understand the day-to-day work of teachers. In doing so, she gained a deeper appreciation of what was required to facilitate teachers' learning of fundamental math, and along with Ellinger, was better situated to embed fundamental math within the workings of a regular elementary school and as part of a professional development framework.

Shinohara and Daehler, like Ellinger and Ma, were interested in deepening teacher content knowledge, this time in science. They saw their goal as "helping K–8 teachers develop a deep understanding of science connected to students and teaching." They speculated that this could best be accomplished on a broad scale by involving teachers in consideration of science dilemmas as represented in cases. They soon found that cases alone were not enough. They had to develop materials for teachers, and they had to pay attention to processes of community building. In doing so, they assumed roles as facilitators, staff developers, and expert guides who knew the content and pedagogy of science well. Here content knowledge alone was not enough. As the project grew, so did content knowledge and the processes for sustaining community.

The above cases all demonstrate that content knowledge develops successfully when it is matched to the context where the work occurs and to the needs of the teachers who participate. Content knowledge occurs when there is an acknowledgement that human resources are essential and when building relationships between and among teachers is included in the agenda. Teachers can best develop new knowledge when content is balanced with community.

CHALLENGES THAT COMMUNITIES FACE

Challenges are endemic to any ambitious social enterprise, and professional learning communities are no exception. Chief among the challenges is navigating the fault line between membership in a learning community, with its collectively developed norms, values, and ways of doing business, and membership in schools and districts that often have very different ways of operating, of engaging in relationships, and agreed-upon social practices.

All of the projects confronted the initial challenge of how to create a space where teachers could leave the norms and habits of their schools at the door and enter into communities where they could share their learning and have a major voice in their own agenda. This was a big transition for teachers who had been so used to being told what to do and to doing it alone; they did not always come willingly to a more collaborative group. The projects had to develop ways to build trust so that participants could participate fully in teaching communities. Some groups planned interactive activities, others modeled collaborative ways of learning, while others invested in materials that encouraged different ways of thinking. For all projects, building trust required a joining of intellectual and personal concerns in ways that engaged participants with one another and with the content. All of this required due diligence to both process and content.

But there were other challenges that were unique to the particular contexts of the work. We have touched on some of these before, but we think they bear mention again. Chief among them were the challenges of wedding community and content, of correcting false assumptions, and of going public. Below, we provide examples of these challenges as they were enacted in the cases.

The Challenge of Wedding Content and Community

Shinohara and Daehler described in detail the challenge of simultaneously creating science learning and creating a community for science teaching. They identified three challenges that occurred throughout their work. First was the need to dispel the existing ideas that teachers held about how to learn science. While the project directors reasoned that science was about producing and interpreting evidence, they found that many teachers had different ideas. They had learned science from a textbook and assumed there were right and wrong answers, similar to the way teachers viewed math in the Elinger case. As a result of this prior experience, the teachers saw science as focusing on knowing the right answers rather than on making hypotheses, engaging in tentative thinking, and using evidence to reach conclusions.

The second challenge concerned the meaning of science ideas. The project directors found that teachers sometimes had memorized a concept without understanding its meaning; they couldn't apply the idea to a different context. The third challenge was the way teachers dealt with the difficulty of science content; they would switch to talk about activities and pedagogy and lose the science ideas altogether. This tendency to veer away from difficult content compounded the issues that project directors faced. It was only when Shinohara and Daehler introduced complex and authentic dilemmas that they were able to meet the three challenges and make progress.

Correcting False Assumptions

The challenge that Moir and Hanson faced occurred within the first few weeks of the New Teacher Center. They and the mentors they selected assumed that being an accomplished teacher was qualification enough to help novice teachers gain teaching competence. However, most mentors did not have clear ideas about how to help new teachers or where to intervene and how. They may have been very good at teaching students in their classrooms, but they were less skilled in articulating their knowledge or in helping people new to the profession gain competence and confidence. The vulnerability of the novice teachers exacerbated the situation. The mentors had to learn how to help their mentees solve immediate problems and enrich their emerging repertoire of knowledge, skills, and abilities. This false assumption about mentor capacities could have led to struggles with relationships and a frantic hopping from problem to problem. The directors of the project had to move quickly to keep this from happening, and so they created the Mentor Forum. They managed to establish the kind of learning community for mentors that the project envisioned for the mentees.

Going Public

Pointer Mace described the unique challenges that professional communities face when teachers go public with their work. In her description of the development of the multimedia websites at the Carnegie Foundation for the Advancement of Teaching, she outlined a model for the future: teachers adding to the knowledge base of their craft by going public with their teaching. The challenges she uncovered were both interesting and novel.

First, teachers struggled with how to take a slice of their teaching and surround it with their thinking. They learned how to do this by going through a sequence of scaffolded activities, from talking with a group about their ideas, to putting it on chart paper so others could see it, to talking about it with an outside audience, and eventually to working on producing a public website. The construction of the sites presented another challenge. Teachers had to learn the criteria for making a good site. They had to figure out how much detail to provide and what information to include about the teacher and her students. They had to decide how to construct a site that was simple in design, but that did not minimize the complexities of teaching, and that was easily and intuitively navigable for the viewer.

SUMMING UP

All of the cases present powerful learnings about professional communities, how they are initiated, structured, and maintained. Taken together, they demonstrate what happens when teachers learn new content at the same time they learn how to participate in learning communities. The cases illustrate the remarkable ingenuity and intelligence that people bring to the challenge of adapting to new contexts and ways of working. They make evident how project directors struggle to provide environments where teachers can develop commitment both to ideas and to relationships. And they speak eloquently of the need to balance content and process. Finally, the cases teach us that the pursuit of competence and community is difficult, but that it is well worth the effort.

From looking at the work of practitioners in the field, we learn that before either competence or community can be developed, participants need to learn to trust one another. Once trust is established, openness about practice follows. Sometimes building community initiates the process; at other times it is the content that does the initiating. In all cases, context matters, as does the capacity of project directors to respond to emerging needs and concerns.

It is our belief that professional communities, such as those highlighted in the five cases, offer real alternatives to the traditional passive "staff development" experiences that many teachers know and have come to dread. These communities are rooted in real teacher practice and in rich content. They confirm that learning something new, whether it be new content, new forms of representation, or new ways of interacting with colleagues, involves a process of unlearning and relearning and requires time and practice. Professional learning communities that join competence and community respond to the intellectual and social needs of educators now and in the future. They hold promise of transforming teaching and learning for both the educators and students in our schools.

References

Appleby, J. (1998). *Becoming critical friends: Reflections of an NSRF coach*. Providence, RI: Annenberg Institute for School Reform.

Ball, D. L. (2003). *Mathematics in the 21st century: What mathematical knowledge is needed for teaching mathematics?* Remarks prepared for the Secretary's Summit on Mathematics, U.S. Department of Education, February 6, 2003, Washington, DC. Retrieved September 15, 2007 from http://www.ed.gov/rschstat/research/progs/mathscience/ball.html

Barnett, J., & Hodson, D. (2001). Pedagogical content knowledge: Toward a fuller understanding of what good science teachers know. *Science Education, 85*(4), 426-453.

Borko, H. (2004). Professional development and teacher learning: Mapping the terrain. *Educational Researcher, 33*(80), 3–15.

Cochran-Smith, M., & Lytle, S. L. (1993). *Inside/outside: Teacher research and knowledge*. New York: Teachers College Press.

Corcoran, T. B. (1995). *Helping teachers teach well: Transforming professional development* [CPRE Policy Brief]. Washington, DC: U.S. Department of Education.

Daehler, K. R., & Shinohara, M. (in press). *Understanding electric circuits*. San Francisco: WestEd.

Goldenberg, C. N., & Gallimore, R. (1991). Changing teaching takes more than a one-shot workshop. *Educational Leadership, 49*(13), 69–72.

Grossman, P., Wineburg, S., & Woolworth, S. (2001). Toward a theory of teacher community. *Teachers College Record, 103*(6), 942–1012.

Hammond, L. D. (1998). Teacher learning that supports student learning. *Educational Leadership, 55*(5), 6–11.

Hammond, L. D., & McLaughlin, M. W. (1995). Policies that support professional development in an era of reform. *Phi Delta Kappan, 77*(8), 597–604.

Hargreaves, A. (1984, October). Experience counts, theory doesn't: How teachers talk about their work. *Sociology of Education, 57*, 244–254.

Hargreaves, A. (1991). Contrived collegiality: The micropolitics of teacher collaboration. In J. Blasé (Ed.), *The politics of life in schools* (pp. 46–72). New York: Sage.

Heller, J. I. (2006). Final evaluation report for *Science Cases for Teacher Learning: Impact on Teachers, Classrooms, and Students, Project Years 2000–2003*. Submitted to WestEd and Stuart Foundation.

Horn, I. S. (2005). Learning on the job: A situated account of teacher learning in high school mathematics departments. *Cognition and Instruction, 23*(2), 207–236.

Hutchinson, Y. D. (2003). *A friend of their minds: Capitalizing on the oral tradition of my African American students*. Retrieved June 11, 2007, from http://gallery.carnegiefoundation.org/collections/quest/collections/sites/divans-hutchinson_yvonne/

Kennedy, M. (1998). *Form and substance in inservice teacher education* (Research Monograph No. 13). Madison: National Institute for Science Education, University of Wisconsin.

Levien, P. (2005). *Why teach and perform Shakespeare? Learning from the bard.* Retrieved June 11, 2007, from http://gallery.carnegiefoundation.org/collections/quest/collections/sites/levien_phil/

Lewin, K. (1951). *Field theory in social science: Selected theoretical papers.* New York: Harper & Row.

Lieberman, A. (2007). *Reflections on professional community in the Carnegie Academy for the Scholarship of Teaching and Learning.* Unpublished paper.

Lieberman, A., & Miller, L. (1992). *Teachers—their world and their work.* New York: Teachers College Press.

Lieberman, A., & Miller, L. (2004). *Teacher leadership.* San Francisco: Jossey-Bass.

Lieberman, A., & Miller, L. (2007). Transforming professional development: Understanding and organizing learning communities. In W. D. Hawley (Ed.), *The keys to effective schools: Educational reform as continuous improvement* (pp. 99–116). Thousand Oaks, CA: Corwin.

Lieberman, A., & Wood, D. R. (2002). *Inside the National Writing Project: Connecting network learning and classroom teaching.* New York: Teachers College Press.

Little, J. W. (1990). The persistence of privacy: Autonomy and initiative in teachers' professional relations. *Teachers College Record, 91*(4), 509-536.

Little, J. W. (1993). Teachers' professional development in a climate of educational reform. *Educational Evaluation and Policy Analysis, 15*(2), 129-151.

Little, J. W., & Curry, M. (2008). Structuring talk about teaching and learning: The use of evidence in protocol-based conversation. In L. M. Earl & H. S. Timperley (Eds.), *Professional learning conversations: Challenges in using evidence for improvement* (pp. 29–42). New York: Springer.

Little, J. W., & Horn, I. S. (2007). "Normalizing" problems of practice: Converting routine conversation into a resource for learning in professional communities. In L. Stoll & K. S. Louis (Eds.), *Professional learning communities: Divergence, depth, and dilemmas* (pp. 79–92). Maidenhead, England: Open University Press.

Loucks-Horsley, S. (1998). JSD forum: I have changed my emphasis. *Journal of Staff Development, 19*(3), 7–8.

Ma, L. (1999). *Knowing and teaching elementary mathematics: Teachers' understanding of fundamental mathematics in China and the United States.* Mahwah, NJ: Erlbaum.

McLaughlin, M. W., & Talbert, J. E. (2001). *Professional communities and the work of high school teaching.* Chicago: University of Chicago Press.

Miller, L. (2001). School–university partnership as a venue for professional development. In Lieberman, A. & Miller, L. (Eds.), *Teachers caught in the action: Professional development that matters* (pp 102-117) New York: Teachers College Press.

Miller, L. (2007). *Reflections on professional community in the Southern Maine Partnership.* Unpublished paper.

Myers, J. (2005). *Living the life of a reader and writer.* Retrieved June 11, 2007, from http://gallery.carnegiefoundation.org/collections/quest/collections/sites/myers_jennifer/

National School Reform Faculty. (1998). *A community of learners in Souhegan High School, Amherst, New Hampshire.* Providence, RI: Brown University Press.

National Staff Development Council. (nd). *Learning strategies and designs.* Retrieved September 25, 2007, from http://www.nsdc.org/library/strategies.cfm

Newman, F., & Wehlage, G. (1995). *Successful school restructuring.* Madison: Center on Organization and Restructuring Schools, University of Wisconsin.

Polya, G. (1988). *How to solve it: A new aspect of mathematical method.* Princeton, NJ: Princeton University Press.

Richert, A. (2007). *Learning about adolescents from teachers who teach them well*. Retrieved March 31, 2008, from http://quest.carnegiefoundation.org/~arichert/

Ruff, W. (1991). *A call to assembly: The autobiography of a musical storyteller*. New York: Viking Press.

Sarason, S. (1996). *Revisiting the culture of the school and the problem of change*. New York: Teachers College Press.

Schön, D. A. (1983). *The reflective practitioner*. New York: Basic Books.

Scott, A. O. (2003, February 9). Destined for failure. *New York Times Magazine*, p. 15.

Seashore, K. L., Kruse, S. D., & Marks, H. M. (1996). Schoolwide professional community. In F. W. Newman (Ed.), *Authentic achievement: Restructuring schools for intellectual quality* (pp. 179–203). San Francisco: Jossey-Bass.

Sherin, M. (2004). New perspectives on the role of video in teacher education. In J. Brophy (Ed.), *Using video in teacher education* (pp. 1–27). Amsterdam: Elsevier Science.

Shinohara, M., Daehler, K. R., & Heller, J. I. (2004, April). *Using a pedagogical content framework to determine the content of case-based teacher professional development in science*. Paper presented at the annual meeting of the National Association for Research in Science Teaching, Vancouver, British Columbia, Canada.

Shulman, L. (1986). Those who understand: Knowledge growth in teaching. *Educational Researcher, 15*(2), 4–14.

Shulman, L. (1987). Knowledge and teaching: Foundations of the new reform. *Harvard Educational Review, 57*(1), 1–22.

Shymansky, J., & Matthews, C. (1993). *Focus on children's ideas about science: An integrated program of instructional planning and teacher enhancement from the constructivist perspective*. Report on the Proceedings of the Third International Seminar on Misconceptions and Educational Strategies in Science and Mathematics. Ithaca, NY: Misconceptions Trust.

Van Driel, J. H., Verloop, N., & Wallace, B. (2007). *Professional Development: Noyce Foundation's Every Child a Reader and Writer Program* (available at insideteaching.org). New York: Carnegie Foundation for the Advancement of Teaching.

Viadero, D. (October 13, 2004). Teaching mathematics requires special set of skills: Researchers are looking for new and better ways of mastering concepts. *Education Week, 24*(07), 8.

Vygotsky, L. S. (1978). *Mind and society: The development of higher psychological processes*. Cambridge, MA: Harvard University Press.

Wallace, B. (2007, July 15). *Every child a reader and writer*. Retrieved November 15, 2007, from http://insidewritingworkhop.org.

Waller, W. (1967). *The sociology of teaching*. New York: Wiley. (Original work published 1932)

Wenger, E. (nd). Communities of practice: A brief introduction. Retrieved January 23, 2008, from http://www.ewenger.com/theory/index.htm

Wenger, E. (1998). *Communities of practice: Learning, meaning, and identity*. Cambridge, UK: Cambridge University Press.

Wood, D. R. (2007). Teachers' learning communities: Catalyst for change or a new infrastructure for the status quo? *Teachers College Record, 109*(3), 699-739.

About the Editors and Contributors

Christine Cziko is currently the Academic Coordinator of the Multicultural Urban Secondary English (MUSE) credential/MA program at the University of California, Berkeley. She has been a middle and high school English teacher for over 25 years in urban schools in New York City and San Francisco. She is a member of the Bay Area Writing Project and is particularly interested in issues of adolescent literacy and the preparation of urban school teachers. She has co-authored a book about supporting struggling readers (*Reading for Understanding*) and has written numerous articles based on her classroom experiences.

Kirsten R. Daehler began her work in science education as a high school chemistry and physics teacher and department chair, where she delighted in her work with adolescents and her fellow science teachers. Upon joining WestEd in 1994, Kirsten served as the lead teacher developer and content expert for the National Board for Professional Teaching Standards. Currently, Kirsten co-directs the Understanding Science project, where she aims to transform the way teachers learn about science and the complex art of teaching science. Kirsten holds a BA in chemistry from Wellesley College and an MA in secondary education from San Francisco State University.

Matt Ellinger currently serves as the director of multimedia development for the Strategic Education Research Partnership. Prior to that, he worked at the Carnegie Foundation for the Advancement of Teaching as a researcher and liaison to teachers on projects with scholars Liping Ma, Ann Lieberman, and foundation president Lee Shulman. His research career follows more than 15 years of experience in schools, both as an administrator and as a teacher. While teaching, he worked as a case writer and consultant at WestEd, where he produced professional development materials and assessments for other elementary teachers.

Susan Hanson has over 20 years of experience in the field of education research and program evaluation. She currently works with Ellen Moir, director of the New Teacher Center at UC Santa Cruz, as a researcher documenting how mentor support systemically leverages teacher talent to develop school leaders and catalyze schoolwide improvement. Specializing in the use of qualitative methodology to understand K–12 schools, Dr. Hanson previously worked at SRI and WestEd on evaluation and policy studies related to teacher development.

Ann Lieberman is an emeritus professor from Teachers College, Columbia University, and is currently a Senior Scholar at The Carnegie Foundation for the Advancement of Teaching. Her recent books include *Teacher Leadership*, published by Jossey-Bass and co-written with Lynne Miller. Her unique contribution has been to go between school and university, embracing the dualities that plague our field—theory/practice; process/content; intellectual/social-emotional learning; policy/practice—and helping to build a more comprehensive understanding of teachers and schools and what it will take to involve them in deepening their work. To do this, she has fashioned a way to be both a scholar and an activist, a practitioner and a theoretician.

Désirée Pointer Mace is an assistant professor of education at Alverno College. Her work focuses on envisioning and inventing ways of representing teaching and learning using new media and online technologies. She has developed multimedia websites of exemplary practitioner inquiry for many years, beginning with her work at the Carnegie Foundation for the Advancement of Teaching. There she created a "living archive" of teaching practice (www.InsideTeaching.org). Pointer Mace taught elementary school for many years as a Spanish bilingual teacher and bilingual resource specialist in the Oakland and San Francisco Unified School Districts.

Lynne Miller has been the director of the Southern Maine Partnership since 1987. She is also Professor of Educational Leadership at the University of Southern Maine, where she held the Russell Chair in Philosophy and Education from 2005–2007. Before joining the USM faculty in 1987, she held a variety of teaching and administrative positions in public schools in Pennyslvania and Indiana. In addition, she served as Assistant Professor of Education at the University of Massachusetts, Amherst, where she was the liaison to the Worcester Teacher Corps and to the Boston de-segregation effort. As a scholar, she has she written widely in the fields of professional learning and school reform; most recently she completed two books with Ann Lieberman, *Teachers Caught in the Action* (Teachers College Press, 2001), and *Teacher Leadership* (Josey-Bass, 2004). She is currently engaged in connecting high school and college faculty in efforts to prepare more students for success in higher education.

Ellen Moir is founder and executive director of the New Teacher Center at the University of California, Santa Cruz. For more than 20 years, she has pioneered innovative approaches to new teacher development, research on new teacher practice, and the design and administration of teacher induction programs. Ellen has received national recognition for her work, including the Harold W. McGraw, Jr. 2005 Prize in Education and the 2003 Distinguished Teacher Educator Award from the California Council on Teacher Education. Ellen is the author of several articles and book chapters and has a produced video series related to new teacher development.

Mayumi Shinohara is a senior research associate at WestEd, where she studies children's thinking in science. Originally trained as a physicist, she is now principal investigator of learning science for teaching with Joan Heller and Judith Warren Little, a large-scale study on the effects of content-rich, practice-based professional development models on teachers, classrooms and students. She is also codeveloping Understanding Science, a case-based professional development curriculum designed to help teachers learn science and examine the ways in which children think about and sometimes misunderstand science ideas.

Index